THE PROCRASTINATION DOCTOR PRESENTS:

Starting Tomorrow©

7 Steps to Lasting Change — Get Stuff Done and Have More Fun!

Kim Kensington, Psy.D.

Starting Tomorrow

7 Steps to Lasting Change — Get Stuff Done and Have More Fun!

Kim Kensington, Psy.D.

Cover clock by Jill Badonsky

Procrastination Press
Copyright © 2015 Kim Kensington

Disclaimer

This book is for your personal enjoyment and education only. While best efforts have been used, the author and publisher are not offering legal, accounting, medical or any other professional advice and make no representations or warranties of any kind and assume no liabilities of any kind with respect to the accuracy or completeness of the contents and specifically disclaim any implied warranties of merchantability or fitness of use for a particular purpose, nor shall they be held liable or responsible to any person or entity with respect to any loss or incidental or consequential damages caused, or alleged to have been caused, directly or indirectly, by the information or programs contained herein. Stories, characters, and entities are fictional. Any likeness to actual persons, either living or dead, is strictly coincidental.

All images are free to use or share, even commercially, according to Google at the time of publication unless otherwise noted.

The information, ideas and techniques in this book are not medical advice or treatment, but rather knowledge intended to assist the reader. It is the responsibility of the reader to seek treatment for any medical, mental or emotional conditions that might warrant professional care.

ISBN: 978-0-9896628-1-9

THE PROCRASTINATION DOCTOR'S SOLUTION
REVIEWS

"I think that every aspect of my life is improved because of the organization skills I learned with this program. This is a great program for people ready to stop procrastinating and get down to business!"

Alison B., Commercial Actress

~~~~~

"Thank you so much!!! The (program) is a must-do for procrastinators. I can only say that it works!...and... The stars and rewards are fun. Kim is 'positively' great, and very supportive. This program works for the ADD/free-spirited types and the extremely detail-oriented (and is not at all like boring seminar/self-help meetings or trips to the dentist)."

Zoey G., Actor/Artist

~~~~~

"Just wanted to reiterate my thanks to you. This really is the first program that has worked for me: for four weeks now, I've been working on my book weekly. HUGE success for me! I've also been able to incorporate it with my other priorities: eat healthy and exercise. It really IS a life-changing [system] in that it makes you start dealing with your life. It finally started me working on my goals instead of worrying about them! It's structured, organized and it works!"

Sarah S., Librarian/Writer

~~~~~

"I LOVED it!!!!!"

Marla C., Producer

"This program made the process of getting organized and motivated into a lifelong habit, not just a quick-fix solution. A very supportive teacher and atmosphere."

Paul B., Actor/Writer

~~~~~

"Dr. Kensington's teaching style is warm, light, and she creates a learning environment that is friendly and progressive. A simple system for getting things done."

Delena K., Sales Coach and Consultant

~~~~~

"I just wanted to thank you for the class—I got heaps out of it. I really enjoyed your acknowledging, accepting and enthusiastic style of leading the class. Thanks again."

J.H.

~~~~~

"I have so struggled with time management, and this is the only overall solution that I seem able and happy to incorporate. I also really like that it challenges me to reward and acknowledge the good work I'm doing and is built on a reward system—not a system of reprimands, sheer discipline, and other such negative reinforcement. The Master List is great at heightening my consciousness about what I WANT to be doing routinely, while the Star Sheet makes me feel so good about contributing daily to the four domains in life most important to me. The sequencing concept with the notion of turning distractions into incentives totally helps keep things prioritized while giving them forward momentum. This program has so helped me conceptualize the four core pillars/domains of my life and put them in balance so that I'm living a healthier, happier lifestyle. So thank you, thank you, thank you, thank you!"

Heidi H. Teacher

Dedication

This book is dedicated to Martin C. Gleich.

My staunchest ally and the most amazing human I have ever met.
Martin, I'm finishing this book because I told you I would.
Thanks for believing in me.

Contents

Introduction

**_Please give a warm welcome_ to Kim Kensington,
a procrastination expert who has trouble finishing what she—**

IN 2005 MY LACK of follow-through and chronic procrastination had reached a breaking point. Though I had managed to finish graduate school and earn a doctorate of clinical psychology, I was unemployed, $60,000 in debt and alone in Los Angeles. For reasons I couldn't understand or change, I struggled to revise my résumé and write cover letters to prospective employers. There were a dozen great business ideas in my head, but I couldn't get them on paper or in motion. I was five months behind on rent and my landlord had threatened me with eviction.

My personal life was also in disarray. I had joined a gym only one block from home, and yet I couldn't seem to get there and work out. Convinced I needed to eat a healthier diet, I'd buy fresh vegetables, only to throw them away a week later, moldy and untouched. After successfully applying for and receiving food stamps, I lost them because I didn't keep up with the necessary paperwork for renewal. A growing, gargantuan pile of mail had taken over my desk.

I even procrastinated on the one thing that kept my interest and passion: acting. I needed an agent, but before reaching out to anyone, I needed new headshots. In order to find the right photographer, I needed to research and interview at least three. Before I did that, however, I definitely needed to lose weight. And on it went.

When I reached out to my family for help, they unanimously decided that they had rescued me one too many times and needed to stop "enabling" me. They told me they were using "tough love" and, doing what they thought was best, declined to bail me out. Procrastination had pushed me past the point of collapse; I was scared witless. The final straw was a bad reaction to my prescription medication and I became extremely dehydrated and disoriented.

Eventually, I managed to work through the medical issues, but nothing else in my life changed. Procrastination was still my constant companion and enemy. In desperation, I paid a visit to my local bookstore in search of a self-help book that would tell me what to do. I was hunting for an upbeat title, such as: "The 28 Day Miracle Solution for Getting Your Act Together: *Forever*."

Truthfully, my bookshelves at home were already filled with how-to books and self-help programs. But I had failed, repeatedly, to get organized, manage my time, sculpt abs of steel, get things done or develop even *one* of those habits of highly effective people.

As I thumbed through book after book, I was discouraged anew. The promising sounding programs from authors of the "just do it" crowd were based on the shaky assumption that their readers possessed self-discipline, perseverance and, of course, willpower. However, those qualities were present for me only in rare, small, brief bursts. I had a pattern I knew all too well.

On Day One, I would throw myself into the program, full of enthusiasm and hope. On Day Two, I would eagerly pick up the book, read the next step and implement it with an abundance of determination and spunk. On the third day, I would pick up the book, then put it down again (on top of one of my many teetering piles) and spend some time researching juice fasts or another topic that now seemed more promising. Then I would take a nap. End of enthusiasm. End of hope.

That day in the bookstore, I remember thumbing through a book on time management. In the index, under the heading "Procrastination," the author offered a one-sentence solution:

"Figure out why you are procrastinating and stop doing it."

Huh? If it was that easy, don't you think I would have done that by now? Not one of those books or programs seemed designed for a person like me.

Then it hit me. People like me didn't write books, let alone books that promised to end procrastination. Well, that's not entirely true. People like me start to write books, but we rarely finish and almost never manage to get them to press and into bookstores. The authors with books on the bookshelves seemed to have no clue as to how help a person like me, create a program we could stick with, much less achieve the kind of success we craved so desperately. Even the books with the intriguing theories about why people procrastinate, glossed over one teensy (but fairly important) piece of the puzzle: *"What do we do about it?"*

In that moment, I made a vow: I would create a program just for "us" — the folks who lacked dependable self-discipline and willpower. Folks who had good intentions but failed, time after time, to follow through. Folks who were discouraged to the point of giving up the good fight. Folks, like me, who yearned to finally get it all together, to be what I call an "Other."

Most of my best friends have been "Others." I hoped that "Other-ness" would be contagious. But if it is, I still haven't caught it. My dear friend, Mary, is an "Other." She never has dirty dishes in her sink. She has the tiniest basket of unopened mail and bills on her otherwise clean kitchen table. There are no file drawers in her home, and she maintains the mythical Inbox Zero! She sends birthday cards and gifts early, practices yoga every day and prepares recipes she saves from *Prevention* magazine.

Mary has money for retirement in IRAs, KEOGHS and other monetary instruments with initials I don't know. She is fabulously thin and fit. Her car is well-maintained and has no stuff in it, other than a single bottle of hand lotion (not even in the trunk)! If she had written this book, she undoubtedly would have deleted the previous 200 drafts of the introduction instead of keeping them "just in case," as I have. She wouldn't have created 200 drafts in the first place.

I would love to have her genetic make-up, but I don't. Oh, how I don't. My gene pool instead is loaded with AD/HD, Attention Deficit/Hyperactivity Disorder — the predominantly inattentive type. What that means for this book is that I am hardwired to understand the struggle with procrastination, disorganization and productivity firsthand. And I know with certainty that relying on willpower is a setup for failure.

While I would love to have morphed into an "Other" so I could share the secret with you, it hasn't happened yet. In the meantime, however, I developed a program that works amazingly well for us, "non-others." This book contains that program.

EXPERT PROCRASTINATOR TO PROCRASTINATION EXPERT

I consider myself a procrastination expert. For 30 years, I have studied; experimented; talked to therapists, coaches and personal trainers; helped clients; and taught procrastination boot camps. I learned that recent research on neuroplasticity (the brain's ability to change by forming new neural connections) indicates that we can change our brain and become more productive by changing our behavior. It all boils down to this:

**"You can rewire your brain by doing something in a
different way over a period of time."**

Okay, so it's not earth-shattering news. After all, habits are something we do again and again over a period of time. But the Procrastination Doctor's Solution turns this ho-hum fact on its ear and delivers it in a form that conquers procrastination for all of us "non-Others."

**Although we can't change our genetics, we can change our brains
(and change our lives) by creating new patterns of behavior.**

As I set out to create this new program, I realized that plenty of people could tell me *what* I needed to do to stop procrastinating and become more productive, but no one explained *how* to do it. I needed practical, step-by-step directions to follow, not just for today and tomorrow, but also for 10 days from now and next month and the month after that. I needed to rewire my brain so that I could do the things that had been so difficult without struggling so much.

I wanted to figure out a system that would install new habits in my life so things would happen automatically. I wanted a foolproof system that didn't depend on my fickle motivation, and one that rewarded even the smallest success, from beginning to end. I wanted to make finding my way to the gym as natural as finding my way to the kitchen.

It was a tall order. How could I succeed where others had missed the mark? Because this wasn't the first time I was 100 percent committed to change, I started with the question:

"What would it take to get a different outcome this time?"

Drawing on my own painful experiences, my psychology background and a renewed sense of determination, I began to answer the question by tapping in to knowledge I already had about myself. My program:

- **Needed to work without extended motivation and/or willpower.**
- **Couldn't involve to-do lists, clocks or trips to the Container Store.**
- **Needed to be simple, fun, habitual and gratifying.**
- **Needed to go beyond crisis-management and establish long-term habits.**
- **Needed a payoff every time action was taken toward my goal, at least until I started to see results (because, let's face it, great abs and inner peace can take a while and patience has never been my virtue).**

I knew the simple, but not easy, formula. I had learned it in graduate school. The challenge would be implementation. And miraculously, I did implement it. I took copious notes on what worked and what didn't. I gave it a trial run, and I was bowled over by the results.

A few months into the program, my apartment was consistently tidy. I was getting up regularly at 5:15 am, writing in my journal, doing 50 minutes of cardio at the gym, walking my dog on the beach, eating a healthy breakfast and washing the dishes after meals. By 10:00 am, I was showered and at my desk working on finances, an income stream and my acting career. By 1:00 pm, I was able to shift gears and indulge in pursuits that felt like luxuries. My "work" was finished. I had created time for creativity. The system was so effective, it was almost creepy. But it was also exhilarating.

One Sunday morning, which was my designated "day off" from working out, I watched in amazement as I laced my shoes to go to the gym. I reminded myself that I did not have to exercise that day. Even when I was halfway to the gym, I told myself that I had full permission to turn around and go home. But I didn't go home. It was as though I was on autopilot. I went to the gym on my "day off" and worked out anyway. My routine had truly become habitual. My procrastination was cured!

Fast-forward to today. It's 10:15 am and I have cleaned the inside and outside windows of my car, washed some of my dishes, started a load of laundry, made coffee and had breakfast, walked my dog around the block, emailed some clients, hung up some clothes and cleaned my dog's ears. So I am following my Procrastination Doctor's Solution to the letter, right?

I have to come clean. My goal this morning was to sit down at my desk and write this introduction. Yes, you read that right: it is still easier to get myself to clean my dog's ears than to do any number of tasks, including working on this book.

I want you to know that at my core, I am still wired as a diehard, off-the-charts procrastinator with serious organization and time-management challenges. I have not found the magic pill, perfect diet, hypnotist, personal trainer, therapist, coach, intuitive, location, career or app to turn me into an "Other." But I have found that we in the "non-Other" category can make changes.

**We can improve our lives and finish important projects
we once thought were out of reach.**

Now that my dog's ears are squeaky clean, I'd like to show you the road to that lofty place.

In this workbook, I will share a collection of tools that you can use in the moment, and a system for creating structure and routine for yourself. If the words "structure" and "routine" make you shudder, don't worry, just a little can make a tremendous difference. The Procrastination Doctor's Solution is effective. The science is solid; you don't have to worry about whether it works. It does. After all, I finished this book!

This is the guide I wish I'd found many years ago. I am thrilled that it has made its way to you. The outcome is all about making serious progress, but the process is all about keeping it fun. Good luck and let me know how it goes!

~The Procrastination Doctor

Turn directly to Part Two and start setting up your personalized program now if reading isn't your thing and/or taking action now makes sense for you. You can always come back later to read this spellbinding explanation (wink, wink).

Part One
"She Blinded Me with Science"

—Thomas Dolby

Dogs, Dragons, and Elephants, Oh, My!

THE BOOK YOU HOLD in your hands starts with the premise that no matter how gung-ho and determined you were when you picked it up, your motivation is bound to fade. By tomorrow it could be gone, pushed aside by another emergency, interesting possibility or novel idea.

Relax. This book assumes sticking with anything for long isn't your forté, it sure wasn't mine, and that's exactly why I designed this program the way I did.

The Procrastination Doctor's Solution is a quick, painless, paint-by-numbers plan that doesn't require grit or even willpower. It will help you create new habits and lock them into place.

It's a plan my client, "Julie," needed desperately. Julie (name changed to protect her) is an extraordinarily talented attorney. When she launched her practice she juggled multiple legal projects easily. But when her caseload increased quickly, she fell straight into overwhelm. Fewer and fewer clients sought her counsel. She won many cases worth literally millions of dollars, but had no cash flow because she had neglected to bill her clients! Nothing she tried worked to solve the problems and she was floundering. Understandably, she was pessimistic. And scared.

Like Julie, many clients come to me after they have been struggling for a long time. They are afraid there is no way out and complain of feeling depressed, hopeless and fearful. Throughout many years of working with clients, I have recognized that many suffer from something psychologists call "learned helplessness."

Learned Helplessness

I remember walking out—or, to be more exact, running out in tears—of an experimental psychology class in which we were supposed to experiment on rats. I'm not wired for that sort of thing, but thankfully a lot of scientists are. They've gone to a lot of trouble to study how animals learn new behaviors and unlearn old ones, so we might as well make use of it.

In Psych 101 we were taught about an experimenter, Martin Seligman, and a famous study. Two groups of dogs received shocks.

- Group one could stop the shock by pressing a lever.
- Group two had no control over when the shocks began and ended.

Nothing the dogs did made any difference. They learned they were powerless.

Then, both groups were put in pens from which they could easily escape the shocks by jumping over a low partition. The dogs in group one jumped over and got away. The dogs from group two did not try to get over the partition. They had given up because they had learned nothing they tried made a difference.

Behavioral researchers have found the same phenomenon among elephants and, yes, humans. When we are frustrated one time too many, we assume the same outcome will occur next time and quit trying. Elephants who are chained to strong iron stakes when young finally give up trying to get away. As adult elephants, huge as a hut, they can still be bound to a stake by a slender rope. They've learned that struggling is useless. They have learned, inaccurately, that they are helpless.

People can be broken this way too. Kids who encounter endless frustration at school might finally stop trying. They expect to fail. Grownups who can't figure out how to stay on top of the mail might conclude they'll never be in control of their finances and accept the chaos and shame of growing debts. They stop believing change is possible.

As a result of your own experiences, you might not believe you can escape your current situation and make real changes. Doubt your doubts. For now, consider that you have more capabilities than you think.

☐**IMPLICATIONS FOR THE PROCRASTINATION DOCTOR'S SOLUTION**

We can break the cycle of learned helplessness by being aware of it, then looking more closely at the reality of our situation.

The Changing Brain: Rewiring/Neuroplasticity

Until recently brain researchers told us that the brain we were born with is the brain we have for life. Over time, they said, our brains would shrink and become less efficient. It was a considered to be normal part of aging. But the best news I've heard as a psychologist is that brains can change for the better. And in fact, we can change the way our brains are "wired" — at any age.

The official word for this amazing possibility is "neuroplasticity." Brain scans, called functional magnetic resonance imaging (fMRI), show that when learning a new task, multiple regions of the brain are activated in a different way than ever before. Performing the new task creates a brand-new pathway among neurons, the cells in the brain that control everything from our breathing to eating an apple.

When new behaviors are repeated over and over, the newly minted neural pathways grow stronger and more robust, increasing the likelihood that you will repeat that behavior. Each time you repeat a behavior, that behavior becomes easier to remember and reproduce.

So by creating new behaviors that we repeat again and again, we can change our "learned helplessness" into "learned industriousness." We can make the switch from being a person who avoids unpleasant tasks to a person who readily jumps into action. We can begin to rewire our brains to create new neural pathways and fresh new habits that help the pounds melt away and, for Julie, get the invoices mailed to clients. The even better news is that you don't have to give up your current fun-loving self in the process. You can have it all!

I compare mapping new neural pathways to taking a hike to a beautiful waterfall. If there is no path to the waterfall, you will have to clear away a lot of brush to get there. A few days later, you want to show your best friend the waterfall, so the two of you follow the same route, cutting a little more brush as you go, making the path easier to navigate. Each time you revisit the waterfall, the brush is trampled a little more, a trail emerges, and your trips get faster and more efficient.

The same thing happens with our brain circuits. The first time we try a new behavior, it's slow-going. We need a lot of encouragement and perhaps some extra incentive to stick with the task. The second time we try that same behavior, it's still difficult, but we feel less burdened. The third, fourth, fifth and sixth times are progressively easier. And the old paths (those procrastination paths) get tangled with undergrowth and become less automatic. Our brain likes the new zippy neural circuits better than the old ones! This is good news: behaviors that might be difficult at first can become easy over time.

☐**IMPLICATIONS FOR THE PROCRASTINATION DOCTOR'S SOLUTION**

Thanks to neuroplasticity, you CAN change your brain. There is scientific evidence that yesterday's procrastination can become tomorrow's good habits with repetition, repetition, repetition.

Behavior Change

When I was in graduate school studying psychology, I was interested in the theories that focused on the deep-seated reasons people do what they do. I wasn't nearly as interested in behavior therapy, where the focus was on symptoms. But as graduation loomed, and I realized that all the insight in the world wasn't doing squat to make me revise my résumé and write cover letters, I did a 180.

The only thing that mattered at the time was actually getting a job. I was beyond caring that my procrastination might be a symptom of deep-seated fears and unresolved childhood issues. I no longer had the time to explore that. I needed to change things right now! I needed to get a job now! I'd deal with my issues, yup, later.

Behavior modification works on monkeys and dogs and rats . . . and people. Teachers who want to stop disruptive behavior in the classroom have used it for years. It is the basis for most addiction-recovery programs that help people unlearn old habits and replace them with new, healthier ones.

Though I've hunted far and wide, I've never seen behavior modification used for help with procrastination. That will change right here in these pages. Using proven methods of behavior change correctly is a virtually foolproof way to get results. I'm going to show you how to use them to work around your procrastination and improve your life. Let's start with a quick tour of how behavior modification makes a difference.

Avoiding Avoidance

When Julie thought about invoicing her clients for the work she had done months ago, she would start to feel sick to her stomach. She imagined her clients opening the bill, making sarcastic comments about her ineptitude and tossing the invoice aside, unpaid. She avoided the unpleasant possibilities by skirting the issue entirely. Unfortunately, her avoidance also had unpleasant consequences for her: no cash flow in her business.

Each time we open the escape hatch and walk away from an anxiety-producing task, we reinforce our procrastination habit. We approach the task, feel awful about doing the task and turn (or run) away. Avoiding the task makes us feel better for the moment, but in the long run, we are setting up a procrastination habit. After several rounds of this pattern, we barely need to think about that hated task before we run away emotionally or physically.

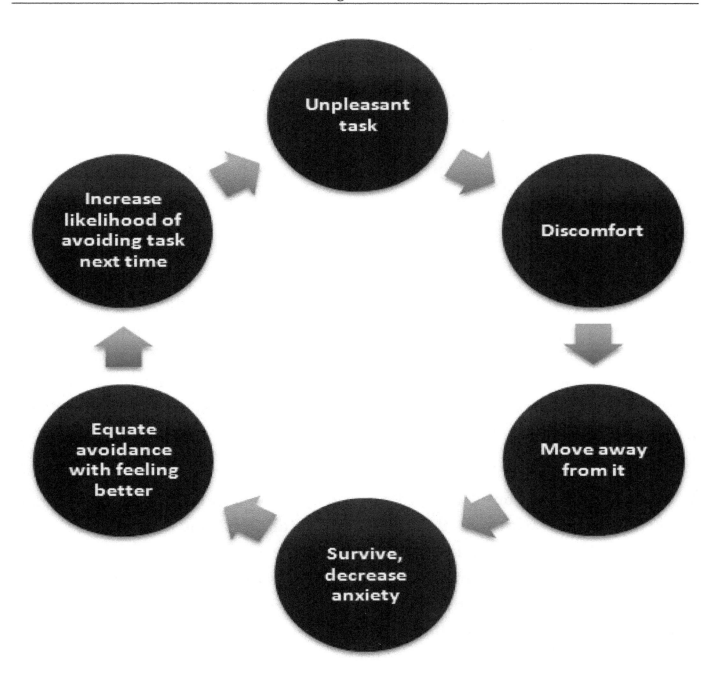

Fear is a basic human emotion. It keeps us safe. We avoid the heat of a roaring fire because we have learned it will sear our tender flesh. But fear can be misplaced and exaggerated in our mind's eye. Tasks such as billing a client for legitimate, completed work take on disproportionate importance. We are convinced that sending the bill might actually be a life-threatening action, so we avoid it accordingly. Logically, we know it is absurd to fear mailing an envelope that contains an invoice, but our brains are quick to adopt unreasoning fear.

Psychologists often treat irrational fears with behavior modification, and we are going to use it in the Procrastination Doctor's Solution as a way to gradually reduce your aversion to doing those much-needed tasks. As an extreme example, let's pretend that you have a fear of dragons.

A traditional psychological approach might take a look at the dragon you fear most to reduce anxiety about the specific components of the monster. *How many scales does she have on her head? How far can her fire-breath reach? Exactly what shade of green is she?* The therapist might delve into the history of your fear of dragons. *When did you first experience a fear of dragons? Did you have a dragon-related trauma? As a child, did your Puff the Magic Dragon action figure fall off a shelf and hit you on the head?*

While that approach can be beneficial, it can also take a long time. We are instead going to practice exposure therapy, a powerful technique used by behavior therapists. This powerful technique brings you face to face with your fear (sending bills to clients) with gradually increasing exposure to the negative emotion associated with it (shame and fear of dismissal). Within a matter of weeks, you will feel less anxiety about those tasks. Your procrastination (which has been protecting you from perceived fearful tasks) will dissipate.

☐IMPLICATIONS FOR THE PROCRASTINATION DOCTOR'S SOLUTION

Gradually facing your perceived fears will help you stop avoiding tasks that previously seemed too difficult or challenging.

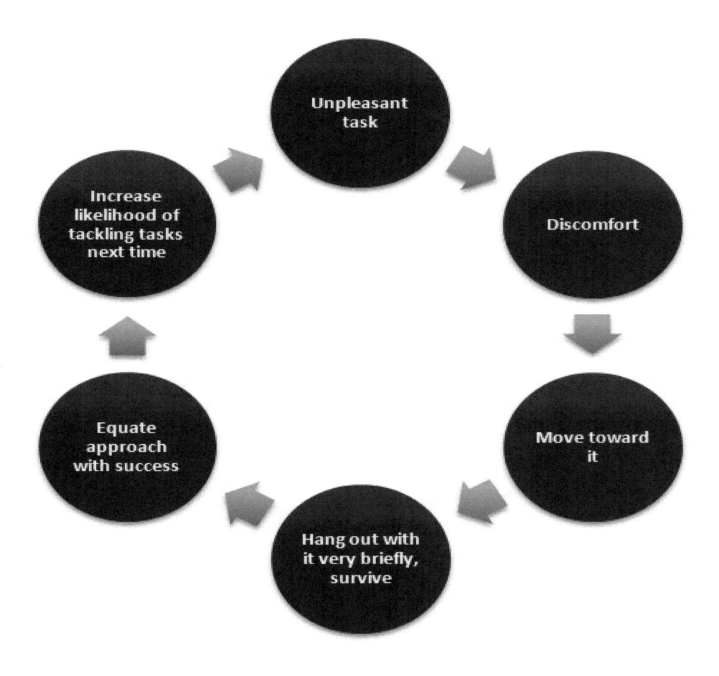

Anchoring the Action

Dr. David Premack was a professor at the University of Pennsylvania when he brought forth his famous theory, the Premack Principle:

"More probable behaviors will reinforce less probable behaviors."

More probable behaviors are the activities we do daily (or habitually) and *less probable behaviors* are the actions we put off until tomorrow (those on which we procrastinate).

Let's say you have an ice cream habit. You eat a bowl of ice cream almost every night (the probable behavior—you *probably will* eat that ice cream). But you know you should eat more leafy green veggies, such as kale or spinach (the less probable behavior—you *probably won't* eat kale under normal circumstances).

To encourage yourself to eat kale, you make a promise: no ice cream until you eat leafy greens. Because you really want your nightly dish of ice cream, you are willing to eat kale before you indulge in Ben and Jerry's. Thus you increase the likelihood that you will eat kale by anchoring it to your ice cream habit.

In behavior modification lingo, the probable behavior (eating ice cream) is known as an ANCHOR for the less probable behavior (eating kale). During the Procrastination Doctor's Solution, we anchor positive, probable behaviors that you already perform (savoring a nightly bowl of ice cream, brushing your teeth, checking your email) with a behavior you want to incorporate into your life (going to the gym, decluttering your office, eating leafy greens).

In Part Two I'll ask you to list some of your daily, regular anchors so we can use them as a tractor beam to attract and implement some of the things you have been procrastinating on for years. Anchors, used well, are pure gold.

□**IMPLICATIONS FOR THE PROCRASTINATION DOCTOR'S SOLUTION**

> You will use anchors (probable behaviors that are already firmly in place) to push through procrastination to do things you want or need (less probable behaviors that seemed out of reach until now).

Get a Cue

Ivan Pavlov is famous for his research with dogs on conditioned reflex. When Pavlov rang a bell, he fed the dogs. Again and again the bell rang and the dogs ate. When dogs anticipate food, they begin to salivate. Over time the dogs associated the bell with food and eventually they would begin to salivate when the bell rang. Pavlov linked two unrelated behaviors: a ringing bell and a drooling dog. The bell was the cue for the dogs to anticipate food and salivate.

The process of conditioned reflex works for us too. We will use Pavlov's experiment to launch a chain of success in the Procrastination Doctor's Solution.

Though it might not involve bells and food, we will deliberately create cues that will trigger us to automatically begin the tasks that we previously avoided.

Cues or triggers are unique to each individual. Julie's trigger that prompts her to eat ice cream might be sitting on the couch to watch television. This association has been repeated again and again so that sitting on the couch automatically triggers heading to the freezer. By repeatedly sitting on the couch, then eating kale, and then eating ice cream, sitting on the couch can become a new trigger for Julie to eat kale!

□IMPLICATIONS FOR THE PROCRASTINATION DOCTOR'S SOLUTION

Noticing and associating triggers already present in your life will ensure easier starts.

Roll Over, Fido

Animals can be taught to do a lot of crazy things. Dogs can learn to find your keys, dolphins jump through hoops, and rats press levers for food. The common thread among all these behaviors is rewards. To firmly establish a behavior, such as finding keys (which is certainly not natural for dogs), trainers use treats, treats and more treats.

We're no different. Our brains are wired for reward. When we anticipate a juicy treat coming our way, the brain releases dopamine, a brain chemical that is linked to feeling good. As we make our way into unfamiliar territory, such as vanquishing procrastination, we need to make sure our brains are happy. That means lots and lots of treats.

Every time we "do it right," for example, overcome our former reluctance to perform a task, we need to give the brain the equivalent of a lollipop. When the brain receives the figurative lollipop, it goes to its happy place. Liking to feel good, the brain wants more lollipops. And more and more. And we provide them . . . right away.

The trick is to reward our brain with a lollipop every single time we take action toward our goal. Like Pavlov's dogs, we reinforce the good feeling of taking action with a treat/lollipop, but it must be done reliably. If you skip a treat here and there, your brain will start to mistrust you. You don't want a mistrustful brain. Trust me.

Unless you truly love lollipops, that's probably not going to work as a treat for your brain. But rewards/lollipops can be whatever you feel good about, such as a cup of tea, reading a chapter in a compelling novel, a new pair of earrings or simply taking 10 minutes to sit in the sun. Whatever gives YOU pleasure is your brain's lollipop.

☐IMPLICATIONS FOR THE PROCRASTINATION DOCTOR'S SOLUTION

Regular, consistent rewards are essential to the success of the program. Without rewards, your brain will rebel, slack off and you might slip back into procrastination mode.

Recipe for Success: Putting It All Together

We know what to do. It's the "doing" that's the problem. It is recommended we eat five servings of fruits and vegetables every day. Vegetables are good for us. So is staying on top of our finances. And flossing. Yeah, yeah, we know. The challenge for some of us is how to get ourselves to do that consistently.

Many parents out there know about Jessica Seinfeld's cookbook, which gives recipes for how to "hide" vegetables in food so that kids unknowingly eat what they would normally refuse. Her recipe for macaroni and cheese includes finely ground cauliflower. She hides beets in colorful pancakes.

The Procrastination Doctor's Solution is like Seinfeld's recipes. We pair things you like doing (those probable behaviors again) with things that are less desirable (such as sending invoices—less probable behaviors) so you eat your mac and cheese cheerfully. It's the spoonful of sugar that helps the medicine go down.

During the next four weeks, we will increase the amount of "cauliflower" in your dish. As a result, you will gradually grow accustomed to being more productive with fewer struggles. Someday, raw cauliflower might even seem delicious to you.

~~~~~

Luis

I'd like to introduce you to Luis, one of my clients who had a long history of procrastination. He completed the Procrastination Doctor's Solution with remarkable results. I share his story so you'll have a sneak preview of what's in store.

Luis was determined to get in shape, but despite his best intentions, he claimed he couldn't find time to exercise. The truth was, Luis really didn't like lifting weights and sweating. He preferred watching TV or talking long walks with Max, his beloved dog.

Luis' goal in the Procrastination Doctor's Solution was to add 30 minutes of exercise to his schedule. Max, his dog, became part of Luis' transformation.

Max was accustomed to a long walk about 5:00 pm each day. That walk became Luis' probable behavior or his ANCHOR for his new exercise regimen.

When it was near five o'clock, Max began following Luis from room to room staring at him, as if to REMIND Luis that Walk Time was here. Then Luis would put on his sneakers and take Max on his walk. Putting on his sneakers became the TRIGGER for him to exercise.

Luis inserted a small amount of exercise immediately before he took Max on a walk. That was his NEW BEHAVIOR.

Since Walk Time was something Luis and Max did every day, whether or not he exercised, it worked as an anchor, but wasn't enough of for a reward. Luis needed something extra for each day that he included his new behavior. Though he often listened to the radio when he walked Max, there was a new podcast that had captured his interest. He used the new podcast as his REWARD, listening to it only after he worked out.

Eventually, the sequence looked like this:

- **Max stares at Luis — REMINDER.**
- **Luis puts on sneakers — TRIGGER.**
- **Luis exercises — NEW BEHAVIOR.**
- **Luis walks Max — ANCHOR.**
- **Luis listens to new podcast — REWARD.**

Though Luis started with just 5 minutes of exercise, at the end of his 28 day program, he was exercising for a full 30 minutes before Walk Time with Max. And he was not locked into a particular workout; as long as he did some form of exercise during that time, he counted it as a success.

- **Luis exercises for 30 minutes — NEW BEHAVIOR SUCCESS.**

By day 28 of the program, Luis' brain was becoming accustomed to its new neural pathways and the entire program was easier to follow. There were plenty of rewards, so his brain was full of dopamine and happy as a clam at high tide.

Unlike the many disclaimers you see on television in the fine print, Luis' results ARE typical and your results might be even better than his.

The Procrastination Doctor's Solution takes a bit of time and some practice to prepare at first, and there's a real danger that you might give up too soon and return to counting carrot cake as a vegetable. Because you aren't relying on grit, self-discipline or willpower, you'll need a really powerful motivator to keep coming back to the test kitchen for 28 days.

Though the podcast was enough to draw Luis to his walks, he needed a much stronger motivator to encourage him to persist through the entire 28 day program. He decided to treat himself to tickets to see his favorite sport team compete if he worked toward his goal at least 24 of the 28 days in the program. He tracked his progress using the Procrastination Doctor's Solution Star Chart, a strong visual reminder that he was making a change in his life.

- **Luis makes modifications and tracks his progress for 24 or 28 days—and receives his GRAND PRIZE REWARD.**

This program is a unique combination of time-tested methods, designed with the chronic procrastinator in mind. You will not only reach your goals, but you will maintain your progress and perhaps venture into new areas of success.

No need to think; the sections that follow contain the how-to, the paint-by-numbers, the step-by-step success plan I promised. Get ready to move from *inaction* to being *in action*. Now let's get started.

Today I will start a project only so I can later abandon it because of my perfectionistic standards.

~Ann Thornhill and Sarah Wells

Part Two
The Procrastination Doctor's Solution

Ready, Set, Go!

I NEED 3 MINUTES of your time right now. Seriously. Don't get up! You don't need a pen, a snack or a drink of water first. I don't care if you are browsing in the library or the bookstore, have made it to the parking lot, or are really jones-ing to see what other people on Amazon.com bought after buying this book.

You might not be able to imagine it, but your current level of determination and commitment is likely to fade. This will leave you dependent on willpower. Let's be savvy and accept that it's easy to get bored, frustrated or distracted. Set yourself up now to persevere through the entire four weeks, long enough to get results.

I don't want you to go any further without promising you will collect a specific grand prize for your upcoming effort. What's it worth to you to transform? $20? $100? $1,000? $10,000? About as much as it would cost to—get a massage? Go to Disneyland with your child? Buy the latest iGadget? Attend the next World Cup? What would you be willing to promise yourself as an investment in your future? You need a really, really good bribe for yourself. What will it be?

Do not skip this step!

If you are totally stumped, list three options. There is a point later in the program where you can change the prize. Promise yourself SOMETHING GOOD! NOW!

Sign this contract with yourself or, if you can't reach a pen, text yourself. If you are feeling particularly brave, tell someone else.

I, _____, *will give myself* _____

for setting up my program and then checking in 24 out of 28 days.

Directions

Okay, you can get a drink of water now. But leave your phone here, facedown, so that you will be drawn back to check for notifications.

The exercises that follow are the backbone of the Procrastination Doctor's Solution. They will help you clarify specific actions and solutions that will make it easier to build the habits that will get you results. The clearer and more specific you are, the higher your success rate will be for making big changes.

You will start by targeting one area of your life and building one new habit at a time so that you grow comfortable with the process. Start small, really commit to making the change and you will see how this program can work. Once you are familiar with the steps, you can use them repeatedly to target multiple obstacles and areas that need change, eventually expanding to all aspects of your life.

The exercise worksheets are reprinted in the appendix and can be copied and reused. While it might be tempting to read the exercises and do them in your head, don't! Research has shown that writing them out is far more effective.

Do each step in order because the process builds on each step. Each step includes exercises to help you fill in a box at the end labeled "The Big Payoff." If you realize you don't need the exercises, you can skip them and go straight to filling in this box. While there is a time guide for each exercise within a step, you can take as long as you want to get to Step Six. You begin collecting stars and your check-ins when you reach Step Six.

Bottling the Magic of Deadlines

If I have 15 minutes to clean before a friend comes over, it's miraculous how much I can get done. If I have a whole weekend to clean, it takes the entire weekend. Just as my stuff fills up my available space, my tasks expand to fill my available time.

Have you noticed right before a deadline, you can often seem to access superpowers? But the deadlines have to be ones you take seriously. Running out of time speeds you up, and suddenly you can shift into rapid-action mode. You also might find yourself thinking more clearly.

If you use and respect a countdown timer, you can access some of that magic. Put yourself into a race against the clock and when the alarm chimes, stop.

IMPORTANT

Each exercise has a specific time limit. As you begin the exercise, I want you to set a timer and make the commitment to stop when the time is finished.

Stopping can be more difficult than it sounds. Time management experts often suggest telling yourself that you will just do something for 5 minutes. The idea is that once you start, you will find a groove and keep going. The problem is you don't dare stop because you never know when you'll get yourself to start again, and you take your action past the point of comfort. If you do too much, the experience becomes a negative one, and it's that much harder to start up next time.

Respect your timer, and it will respect you.

If you promised yourself to exercise for just 5 minutes and then spent an hour on the rowing machine, you broke your promise. Why would you trust yourself next time when you say you're going to do something for only 5 minutes?

By stopping when you said you would, you are taking the first step toward rebuilding trust and integrity with yourself. And it makes it much easier to start next time!

Supplies

Before you go through the exercises in the rest of the book, you might want to gather a few props to make the exercises more effective. But don't let yourself get distracted with elaborate preparations. The most important thing is to channel the energy you have now for success — later.

Timer

Good time management starts with a timer. Or ends with a timer. Oh, for Pete's sake, use a timer! The one on your phone is okay, but an app that gives you warning alerts at 10 minutes and again at 5 minutes before your deadline is ideal.

If you prefer to buy a separate timer, I've included links to my favorite inexpensive versions in the appendix of the book.

Stickers or Stars

Track your progress visually — it is one of the most effective techniques you can employ. Yes, you could draw a star on your Procrastination Doctor's Solution Star Chart (to come) to keep track of your accomplishments, but somehow that doesn't give the same sense of satisfaction as adhering a shiny smiley face, a dollar sticker, or a shimmering star. Even if it reminds you of kindergarten, use that Star Chart and get yourself some stickers before you reach Step Six.

Most drugstores, grocery stores, office supply stores, and dollar stores sell stickers, and they don't cost much. Get some.

Tip

Have as lighthearted and playful an attitude as possible about this process. If you keep it fun, you'll keep at it!

I, _____, will give myself

_____

when I complete this 28 day program.

Date: _____

Time: _____

Signature: _____

Don't compluticate the sitiation.
~Grandpa

Step One: Mind Fields

Simplify
Get It Out
Piling System
Finalists
The Big Kahuna

Simplify

PRODUCTIVITY EXPERTS sometimes suggest taking an extraordinarily complete and thorough inventory of tasks that need to be completed. This might involve going through all your to-do lists and going through each room in your home. That's when I get overwhelmed and give up.

Your first step will be to sift through this huge pile of "to do's" that might be swimming in your head and simplify where to start. If you can already identify the area of your life in which you most want to make change, feel free to fill in the box below and jump to Step Two. If you don't have that clarity yet, follow the steps below — it shouldn't take more than 15 minutes. And have fun with it!

Get It Out

Exercise 1a

Time limit: 5 minutes

First things, first: let's do a quickie clearing out of that brain of yours and start making some space. In a free-form, unorganized way, write whatever you'd like to accomplish that comes to you in the next 5 minutes. You aren't aiming for a complete or perfect list. This is not the time to be realistic. It's okay to be vague! Get as much as possible out of your head now, and we'll make sense of it — wait for it — later!

The one caveat is that these changes cannot be what you wish to change in another person. You only have control over yourself.

Commit to doing a messy and mediocre job here. Tell the critical gremlin in your head to go play a video game — you don't need her/him right now!

Examples

- Get in shape.
- Make more money.
- Get organized.
- Run a 5K.
- Write a novel.
- Become famous.
- Meet my true love.
- Get out of debt.
- Lose 10 pounds.
- Be nicer to my sister.
- Make some new friends.
- Stop being so messy.
- Get out of bed earlier.
- Make the bed.
- Floss daily.
- Stop losing my keys.
- Clean up my office.
- Shred the boxes of paper.
- Remember Grandma's birthday.
- Eat healthier food.
- Drink more water.
- Pay bills on time.
- Write every day.

Write as fast as you can, dumping the things you want to do or change out of your head and onto the paper. Do not censor or correct. Just write! Set your timer for 5 minutes. **GO!**

_____

_____

_____

_____

_____

_____

_____

_____

_____

_____

_____

Piling System

Exercise 1b

Time limit: 5 minutes

Now *generally* sort the giant "pile" of ideas. Not everything will fit in the categories you choose, and some might fit in multiple categories. That's totally fine. None of this is permanent or binding!

For example, the items in the list above might fit into categories like this.

Example

Health and Fitness	Diet and Nutrition	Home Environment
Lose 10 pounds Bench press 120 lb Run a 5K Floss daily	Eat healthier foods Drink more water Take vitamins and herbs	Invite people over any time Declutter Find things easily

Feel free to write in the boxes below or choose another way that works for you. Set your timer for 5 minutes. **GO!**

Job and Career	Finances	Health and Fitness	Diet and Nutrition
Creativity	Spiritual	Family and Friends	Intimate Relationships
Personal Growth	Home Environment	Office Environment	Miscellaneous

Finalists

Exercise 1c

Time limit: 1 minute

Next, circle four categories that matter most to you—for any reason. You can do this **intuitively** (you just know what they are) or **logically** (which categories have the most items, have the greatest degree of urgency, affect your self-esteem the most, wreak havoc on many other areas of your life, etc.).

Write the category names below. Set your timer for 1 minute. **GO!**

1. _____

2. _____

3. _____

4. _____

The Big Kahuna

Exercise 1d

Time limit: 1 minute

Making one change often triggers a cascade of positive changes. The key here is to teach you the method and have you experience success with it. Ultimately, you might want to address other life categories, and you will be able to do so using the Procrastination Doctor's Solution. For now, since virtually all experts agree that you should only try to change one thing at a time, let's make your first change count!

In which of those categories will taking daily action bring you the most satisfaction, have the greatest likelihood of creating a snowball effect and get you the biggest bang for your energetic buck? Taking consistent action in this category will be your first focus for the Procrastination Doctor's Solution.

Bang-for-Your-Buck Habits

In my experience, the habits that seem to provide the most bang for your buck almost always fall into these four categories:

1. **Exercise.**
2. **Personal growth:** spiritual, prayer, reading the Bible, reading the Big Book, meditation, therapy or counseling, reading self-help books.
3. **Creative self-expression:** doing something soul-satisfying, enjoyable and important to you that you usually put off because you haven't done what you "should" do first (for example, journaling, morning pages, writing poetry, playing music, making art, learning something new, baking, gardening, etc.). This does not include things that manage to sneak into your day anyway (those are anchors) such as TV, Facebook, reading blogs, getting lost in fiction, shopping.
4. **Tidying up a messy space:** desk, kitchen drawer, garage, bedroom.

Look at your Finalists list (Exercise 1c) and choose one category with which to start. What gives you the most anxiety? Where do you have the most unfulfilled dreams? What bugs you every day? Choose based on what you think/guess will feel the best to change. Put the name of the category you picked in the box below.

The Big Payoff
The category in which I most want to make change right now is:
Give it a fun, playful, appealing name if you want.

Congratulations! You have completed Step One: Mind Fields.

I had so many lists, I had to rent a storage unit.
The code to get in is on one of those lists.

Step Two: "To-Do"-ing It Differently

Plan Not to Plan
Success Time
Training Schedule

Plan Not to Plan

Time management and productivity books usually advise planning ahead, making outlines and deciding which specific actions should be taken and in what order. Frequently they suggest making a timeline and scheduling preliminary deadlines. This is a logical and linear approach that apparently works for many people, but the rest of us definitely need another way.

I can burn through a crazy amount of time plotting what I will do and when I will do it, but that rarely translates to action. I get bogged down and overwhelmed with the mere idea of all those tasks ahead of me, and by then I'm sleepy. So instead of creating lists, mind maps, timelines, vision boards, outlines and prioritized to-do lists, you are going to plot how to consistently spend time focusing on what matters most.

Honoring Effort

Time + Effort = Results

Success can be measured by input (time and effort) or by output (tasks that can get crossed off a list).

Output: Apply to ten jobs.

Input: Spend an hour on career advancement.

If it took an hour to reformat your computer because the hard drive crashed, you failed by an output measure but succeeded by an input measure. Failure is not a rewarding feeling at all, and it's that feeling that contributes to feeling helpless and makes us avoid our to-do list even more.

Measuring by input gives us so much more control over the one thing we can control—ourselves. Therefore, we greatly increase the odds of feeling that we succeeded, which makes the next day (and the next) easier.

Luis, my client from the last section, really wants to work out but can't find the time or energy to do so. He wants to add 60 minutes of exercise to his daily routine, but jumping from zero to 60 minutes of exercise each day is a set-up for more TV watching. And since Luis hates lifting weights, forcing himself to pick up dumbbells will lead to the same result: no result at all.

The Procrastination Doctor's Solution has a better idea. Instead of beating your head against that same wall again and again, we take a different tack. Rather than a rigid to-do list that requires specific actions, for example, "Ride my exercise bike two miles at 8:00 am," you will make progress toward your goal in a more flexible manner.

Luis' current category of focus was "Health and Fitness" (from Step One). There are a variety of exercises that fit within that category. Lifting weights is one of them, certainly, but so are digging in the garden, riding a bike, jumping on a trampoline, walking on a treadmill and running up and down stairs.

The idea is to open up the field of possibilities so that you have many avenues through which to succeed. When Luis' dog, Max, stared at him (giving him a strong hint that it was Walk Time), Luis put on his sneakers, then did something, ANYTHING within the Health and Fitness category. He might open a fitness app on his phone and do a few push-ups. He could pop in a yoga DVD and strike a pose. Anything within his chosen category counts as success (and earns the right to put a sticker on your Star Chart, which is coming up soon).

You do not have to specify exactly what actions you will take each day, instead, you get to choose how much time you will spend on the category you chose in Step One. How much time? Jump into your next quick exercise:

Success Time

Exercise 2a

Time limit: 1 minute

Do you have a sense of how much time you would ultimately like to spend attending to this priority each day? Okay, now put it in the blank space below along with your chosen category:

My Category is: _____

My TARGET goal is to work on my category for

_____minutes/hours/day

Training Schedule

Exercise 2b

Time limit: 2 minutes

When you work out with weights to build muscle, you start with a low number of repetitions. As you get stronger and your muscles adapt, you add reps. In preparing for a marathon, you gradually add miles to your training regimen. In both cases, you are building stamina and strength.

You will do the same by dividing the amount of time you want to spend on your goal into four—not coincidentally the number of weeks of the Procrastination Doctor's Solution! You will start with the smallest amount of time so that you begin to integrate this novel action into your current schedule. Then, each week, you will add 25 percent more to your Time Block. At the end of four weeks, you will be all the way to your target time. Confused? Here's an example.

My Category: Health and Fitness

My Target Time Block: 60 minutes

So 60 divided by 4 is 15 minutes — that becomes your incremental Time Block.

> Category: Health and Fitness
> Week One: 15 minutes
> Week Two: 30 minutes
> Week Three: 45 minutes
> Week Four: 60 minutes

Now it's your turn.

Decide on your ideal Target Daily Time Block, the amount of time you are willing to devote to your chosen category. Then divide it by four and do a wee bit of math:

The Big Payoff

End Goal: _____ min/day

Week 1: minutes = 25% of your target = _____min

Week 2: minutes = 50% of your target = _____min

Week 3: minutes = 75% of your target = _____min

Week 4: minutes = 100% of your target = _____min

In week one, my goal is to focus on _____ for _____ minutes a day.

Caveat: Don't bite off more than you can chew. You don't want to burn out (been there, done that) or worse, quit.

Congratulations! You completed Step Two of the Procrastination Doctor's Solution. Let's move on to Step Three: choosing your anchor.

I keep missing my twelve-step meetings.
Where is the program with one step?
~One of Kim's clients

Step Three: Anchors Away

Choose "When" and Develop a Routine
My Anchor List
Trigger Happy
Make a Sandwich
POP Reminder

Choose "When" and Develop a Routine

EVER TRIED TO SCHEDULE everything you intended to do for a day (or week)? "Wake up at 6:30, exercise 7–8, eat, shower, leave by 9, answer emails 9:30–10, return calls 10–10:30, etc."

Without much structure, basing your schedule on the clock can be an exercise in futility. What if you snooze one too many times past your overly optimistic new wakeup time? Your whole day is shot and you're not even out of bed! Or what if your boss calls you (unscheduled) first thing in the morning with an urgent request? Your carefully mapped-out plan is out the window. It is just too easy to feel doomed, hopeless and far behind before you even begin.

On the other hand, without structure, we tend to drift and shift directions as though we had sails in the wind. And the things that aren't getting done probably don't have deadlines, so they get pushed aside. Just as organizers tell us that our possessions should have a place, so too should the things in life we want to do. But what if, instead of constructing an elaborate new schedule, we develop a sequence of actions?

Finding an Anchor

No matter how disorganized or unstructured your life might be, there are probably things you do without fail every single day. These actions offer possible anchors to which you will attach your Time Block.

An ideal anchor (refer to Part One for more information) is something that you can do whenever you finish. It is something that is pleasant but not urgent.

In the next exercise, think through your typical day or week and write down activities you end up doing most days. Some of these will be time sensitive (pick Joey up at 12:30 pm), while others will be actions you repeat throughout the day. List as many as possible to start. As the list evolves, keep an eye out for activities you look forward to and enjoy.

Example List of Possible Anchors

- Check email.
- Pick up kids.
- Shower.
- Go to the mailbox.
- Follow Twitter.
- Watch the news.
- Take out trash.
- Call a friend.
- Make coffee.
- Feed pets.
- Meditate.
- Prepare meals.
- Walk the dog.
- Watch TV.
- Do dishes.
- Workout.
- Play a game.
- Nap.
- Read a blog.

Tips for Choosing an Anchor for Your New Habit Sequence

- Look for an anchor that occurs in roughly the same physical location. Example: check bank balances before checking Facebook.
- Look for an anchor that makes sense in relationship to what you will be focusing on. Examples: exercise before shower, or evening routine before putting on PJs.
- Choose an anchor that tugs or pulls you toward it. Checking email or Facebook makes a fabulous anchor, because it has reinforcing and rewarding properties that lure you toward it.
- Choose an anchor that gently nags. Walking or feeding a dog works well, because most dogs will follow their owners and stare at them when it's meal time or playtime.

Anchor List (a)

Exercise 3a

Time limit: 6 minutes

Think through your typical day or week and write down activities you do consistently, however small, that could possibly be used as an anchor. Don't edit yourself at this point—just write down everything that comes to mind. Set your timer for 6 minutes. **GO!**

_____

_____

_____

_____

_____

_____

Anchor List (b)

Exercise 3b

Time limit: 2 minutes

Now look at your full anchor list and highlight or circle the anchors that you enjoy the most and that occur daily or several times per day. Set your timer for 2 minutes. **GO!**

Anchor List (c)

Exercise 3c

Time limit: 1 minute

The most effective anchors are those that are pleasing to do and that you look forward to doing. You want the anchor to be something you can do after completing your Time Block, so that it reinforces you taking action.

Now choose one anchor from the list above that you can tie to your Time Block. Set your timer for 1 minute. **GO!**

My anchor is: _____

Trigger Happy

What if we could make starting a task automatic? Think back to Pavlov and his dogs: Pavlov rang the bell and the dogs started to drool in anticipation of food. One action can be made to trigger an automatic, unrelated action making it a conditioned response.

Finish a meal. ☐ Wash the dishes.
Arrive at work. ☐ Plan your day.
Stumble out of bed. ☐ Put on workout clothes.

Do you remember Luis and his dog, Max, from Part One? Luis made the commitment to work out for a few minutes each day before he walked Max.

After a while, starting to workout became automatic because Luis had established a trigger: Max would stare at Luis because it was time to go out, which activated Luis to put on his sneakers and do his workout ASAP so he could get to the important stuff — Max.

Looking for Triggers

The sequence you are establishing is: Trigger □ Time Block □ Anchor.

In order to set this sequence in action, you must identify a trigger. Look for an action that comes right before your anchor (for example, right before you check Facebook, you usually get coffee and then sit down at your desk). Sitting down at your desk for the first time in the morning would make a great trigger.

A note about triggers: use physics and location. If planning your day will occur at your desk, look for a trigger that has you at your desk.

Take out all the space between the trigger, your Time Block and the anchor. Using "get coffee" as a trigger might be troublesome if you frequently get stopped in the hall by coworkers before you get back to your desk. Placing the cup on the desk, however, would work.

Make a Sandwich

Exercise 3d

Time limit: 3 minutes

Think about your anchor and what you do immediately before starting it.

Before I _____ (write in anchor), I
_____(trigger). Your Time Block goes between these two events.

Original Sequence
Trigger: Dog stares at me.
Anchor: I walk my dog.

New Sequence
Trigger: Dog stares at me.
New Behavior: Workout.
Anchor: Walk dog.

POP Reminder

While this is all logical, there is still a problem: remembering to disrupt the old pattern and squeeze in something new. This calls for some creativity. At the beginning, as a failsafe, you are going to set up an extra reminder. I call this a POP (point of performance) reminder.

You might be familiar with the "out of sight, out of mind" problem. Perhaps you have been known to set things in front of your door in the hope that you'll remember to take them with you.

Putting stuff in front of your door is a great example of a POP reminder. You have placed the reminder where you need it.

In the beginning you'll need a reminder that is really hard to ignore. It is too easy to step over things and walk out the door empty-handed.

For example, if your new habit is to sit down and plan your workday each morning when you arrive at work, you could put a sheet of orange paper on your desk chair that says "Plan the day!" In the morning when you sit down, you have an obtrusive, tactile POP reminder. Reminders that engage your sense of touch seem to work best (less likely that you'll go around or stop noticing them).

POP Reminder

Exercise 3e

Time limit: 3 minutes

Think about a POP reminder that will remind you to do your Time Block. Where does the reminder have to be located so that you do not overlook or ignore it?

My POP reminder is _____.

Example

Put a hanger on your pillow to remind you that you are developing the habit of putting your clothes away before bed.

Remembering the Reminder

Most advice I've been given, and most self-help books I've read, skip a step (or two or three) for the way my brain works. Even if I put a hanger on my pillow the first night, the odds of my remembering to do that the following morning is extremely slim.

Not only do they assume I will suddenly and repeatedly initiate an action I have a long history of not initiating, they assume I will even remember my intention to do it. Hence, this program—and the next section.

Do not underestimate the power of ingrained habits. To establish a new habit, you must interrupt an existing sequence of actions. It's okay to make your life easier and free up some brain space with reminders.

Examples

If you always leave work at 5:00, set a recurring alarm on your phone for 4:55 that says "put orange paper on seat," so that your POP reminder is in place for tomorrow morning when you arrive.

If you leave work at varying times, but always take your laptop, store the orange paper under the laptop. When you pick up the laptop at the end of the day, there's your orange POP reminder on your desk.

If possible, set that reminder right now! If it needs to happen in a certain location, set a recurring geo reminder app to go off each time you arrive.

Now you can fill in your own New Behavior Sequence in the chart below.

The Big Payoff: Action Sequence and Reminders	
My Time Block is:	_____ minutes a day
Focusing on:	
My anchor is:	
My trigger is:	
My POP reminder will be:	
My reminder to set my POP is:	

Congratulations! Going forward, much less thinking will be required! You've figured out what you will be doing. Now let's talk about the good stuff: rewards!

I have a right to use bribery to get my needs met.
~Ann Thornhill and Sarah Wells

Step Four: Roll Over, Fido

Make Productivity Rewarding
Brainstorm Rewards
The Chosen Few
Snausages
Promises, Promises
The Whole Shebang

Make Productivity Rewarding

Snausages (Motivation)

TEACHING A DOG TO roll over involves several steps. And no self-respecting dog is going to do any of them unless you make it worth it. To learn something new, each behavior along the way needs to be reinforced immediately, each and every time it is performed. Snausages work well for my dog, but you might prefer something else.

Dopamine (Reinforcements and Rewards)

Research has shown that dopamine, the neurotransmitter that makes us feel good, is released more in *anticipation* of receiving a reward than when we actually receive it. Your Procrastination Doctor's Solution is going to be chock-full of anticipation and hits of dopamine.

The treats you choose for yourself must be as good as possible because they are standing in for internal motivation and willpower. These external motivators are temporary. Once you start seeing results and have momentum and the support of habit and routine, you won't need them. But for the next four weeks, they are essential.

Your rewards can be big or small. As long as you want them, they will work. As a general rule, it is best not to reward yourself with food. In this step, you will brainstorm rewards to give yourself each day that you complete your Time Block, as well as juicier inducements that you earn each week.

Let's look back at Luis. He wanted to get in great shape and his new habit was to dedicate time each day before he walked Max. His long-term motivation would come from the rewarding feelings he would get from feeling better about his fitness and appearance.

While he enjoyed walking Max (anchor), he needed an immediate reward that he got only when he completed his Time Block. As part of his reward system, he chose to listen to his favorite podcast only on days he worked out. His Week One prize was a subscription to an ad-free streaming service. This increased the appeal of his reward and supported his plan. It was a little treat, that increased the dopamine in his brain and his mood. He established an association between working out and feeling good immediately as a result and increased the likelihood he would continue.

Brainstorm Rewards

Exercise 4a

Time limit: 10 minutes

Write down anything that feels like a reward to you, large or small. Experiences, a moment to yourself, things you want to buy for yourself, a morning to sleep in — whatever qualifies as a treat to you.

Sample Treats

Here are some ideas to get you started. There are many more in the appendix. Feel free to highlight, copy, cut, paste, add, and subtract to this list! Cut out pages from catalogues to add to your wish list. The more you want them, the more power they have to motivate you.

Home

- Fragrant candle
- New cabinet knobs

Health/Fitness

- Activity tracking gadget
- New workout clothes

Office Organization

- An app that scans receipts
- Session with a professional organizer

Self-Care

- Meditation app
- Massage

Play

- Lunch with friends
- Movie, concert or game tickets

Mental Health

- Adopting a pet
- An audio book

Set your timer for 10 minutes. **GO!**

_____

_____

_____

The Chosen Few

Exercise 4b

Time limit: 3 minutes

Now choose four items/activities from your big list that feel worth working for. It's great to choose ones that support your goal (for example, if you're trying to get into shape, you could reward yourself with a new fitness game for your home console). Do not choose goodies you would give yourself anyway. These need to be special and things you'd be willing to put off getting for a few weeks—just in case.

My Four Weekly Prizes

Week One Prize: _____
for completing six Time Blocks

Week Two Prize: _____
for completing five Time Blocks

Week Three Prize: _____
for completing five Time Blocks

Week Four Prize: _____
for completing five Time Blocks

You might have noticed Week One asks you to complete six Time Blocks, while Weeks Two through Four only five. That is because you are shooting for 21 trials during your Procrastination Doctor's Solution. This amount is often thought to be sufficient to form the basis of a habit.

Snausages

Exercise 4c

Time limit: 6 minutes

There are three different categories of goodies: weekly rewards, daily reinforcers and the Grand Prize. The daily and weekly ones are earned for actively working on your target category for your chosen amount of time.

Daily Treats

Here are a few ideas of rewards that you can give yourself the moment you complete your Time Block:

- Take a turn at your "Words with Friends" game.
- Light a special aromatherapy candle.
- Play a specific song (that only gets played immediately after Time Block).
- Apply special hand lotion.
- Check game scores, Facebook, stocks, etc.

You can use the same treat each time or vary them as long as you decide in advance (remember dopamine comes from anticipation so you need to be specific.) Write down a few items that you can use as immediate reinforcement after completing your Time Block every day:

_____

_____

_____

_____

You can revise or add to this list at any time. You will reward yourself with a predetermined (this is important!) treat each time you complete your Time Block. No exceptions!

Example

Camelia used the Procrastination Doctor's Solution to ensure her home was always tidy enough to comfortably invite in guests. In Week One, she used walking through her front door as the Trigger *for a* Time Block *dedicated to the category she named "Order." She would tidy, organize or clean for 15 minutes prior to having her traditional afternoon tea, which served as her* Anchor.

Camelia loves aromatherapy and used lighting one of her favorite aromatherapy candles immediately after finishing her Time Block *as her immediate* reinforcement. *Her Week One* reward *earned by completing five* Time Blocks, *was an aromatherapy diffuser and a variety of oils. The following week, each time she finished her* Time Block, *she treated herself to a different scent. For her Week Two REWARD, she "splurged" on a line of all-natural, aromatherapy cleansers. She enjoyed using them and this increased the likelihood that she would maintain her newly developed habit of doing a* Time Block *of tidying each day when she came home from work.*

The Grand Prize, Revisited

You can earn your Grand Prize even if you don't do a single minute of your Time Block. Wait, what?

The Grand Prize is for your effort. It is for overseeing your Procrastination Doctor's Solution, hanging in here for the entire four weeks, learning the method and experimenting with solutions for what normally derails you. It is for creating a routine and a space in your life to do what is important to you, with maintenance built-in. It's for not giving up— no matter what!

Completing this 28 day program means staying engaged with it, monitoring your progress and making adjustments as necessary. If you don't do your Time Block, but do try to figure out what happened and how to increase the odds of your success the following day, you get a program star. You earn your Grand Prize by collecting 24 out of a possible 28 program stars.

Promises, Promises

Exercise 4d

Time limit: 12 minutes

Pre-Commitment

If possible, go ahead and do what you can, right now, to ensure you will receive your Grand Prize—invite friends to lunch on a given day, schedule a massage, book a (refundable) night at a hotel, preorder the new iGadget, etc. Make it real. It is too easy to convince ourselves we don't really deserve it, or to put off scheduling it until it seems silly and irrelevant.

Commit now, while it still feels far away, and you still feel committed and optimistic. Given that depending on willpower and intrinsic motivation already has a bad track record, set yourself up with a different source of juice, an alternate incentive for following through with your Procrastination Doctor's Solution! Do this now!

At the beginning of Part Two, I promised that you would have a chance to revise your Grand Prize if you were struggling to make a decision. Here is your chance.

Grand Prize
The Grand Prize I promise to give myself for tracking my progress for 24 out of 28 days is:

The Whole Shebang

Exercise 4e

Now let's put the four pieces of the Procrastination Doctor's Solution together so you can see the full picture:

- Step One: Identify the first area of your life in which you want to develop the habit of consistent action (Category).
- Step Two: Identify how to measure it (Time Block).
- Step Three: Identify the anchor, trigger and POP reminder.
- Step Four: Identify the rewards.

I am creating change in this area of my life:

_____

****

I aim to take action on it for _____ minutes on most days.

****

I will start automatically after this trigger: _____. My reminder will

be _____, and I will put it/create it

by_____.

****

My anchor is: _____.

Each time I complete my Time Block, I will reinforce my action by getting

_____ or doing _____.

****

When I finish one week, I will reward myself with:

_____.

****

For successfully completing 24 out of 28 days, I earn this Grand Prize

_____.

That's Step Four. In my opinion, you have done the hardest work already—you made a lot of decisions. Congratulations!

Sorry to be late. I was teaching my class on time management, and it totally ran over.

Step Five: A Star Is Born

Prepare to Launch
Checklist, Take One
Gold Star!

IF I'M TRYING TO go to the gym, and I discover that I don't have any chilled water, or my iPhone needs to be charged, or I didn't download the latest episode of *Breaking Bad* or I can't find any clean socks, all bets are off. It is astonishingly easy to throw in the (still clean) towel and tell myself I'll go tomorrow. Take a cue from pilots who have a comprehensive checklist to get airborne without a hitch.

Prepare to Launch

Checklist

I am still amazed by how much unconscious resistance and mysterious defeat results from the organizational challenge of remembering, finding, and assembling the "stuff" needed for the job.

By making a quick list of what needs to be in place to execute the new action, you can eliminate a major hidden obstacle. Whenever possible, prepare for next time on the heels of completing your Time Block. Right after you work out, and are experiencing why it feels worth the trouble, set yourself up for your next workout.

Examples

Category: Become a *New York Times* bestselling author

Time Block: 30 minutes doing anything that moves you toward completing current novel
What will you need?
Will you need to print? *Make sure there is paper and ink.*
Will you need your laptop?
Will you need coffee? *Preset the coffee maker to automatically brew around the time you intend to write.*
Will you need room at the table to work? *Clear a space.*
Will you need to feed your cat first? *Don't mess with your cat! Schedule your writing after your cat's breakfast and put a POP reminder on the cat food container.*

Your Checklist might look like this:

- Check paper/ink supply.
- Preset coffeemaker.
- Clear a space to work.
- Charge laptop tonight.
- Pack charger tomorrow.
- Put reminder note "Go Write!" back on cat food container.

Category: Beautiful Home

Time Block: 5 minutes doing any related activity after coming home from work

Will you remember? *Put timer on the surface you see when first entering your home. Ask Siri to set a geo reminder for you to tidy up when you get home.*

Will you lack the energy? *Have Spotify cued to fun, energetic song and place remote next to door.*

Will you be hungry when you get home? *Place box of raisins by front door or in car.*

Your Checklist might look like this:

- Timer
- Siri
- Remote
- Raisins

Category: Spirituality

Time Block: Meditate for 10 minutes before morning shower

Your Checklist might look like:

- Meditation pillow
- Timer
- Incense
- Matches
- Reminder clipped to shower curtain

Checklist, Take One

Exercise 5a

Time limit: 15 minutes

Now close your eyes and visualize yourself going through the entire sequence of actions and then feeling awesome at the end. As you visualize, see if you can predict possible obstacles or opportunities for derailment. Make a list of everything you need to have and to do in order for your Time Block to happen without a hitch. What can you do ahead of time to increase your odds of success? Add it to the list! You can rearrange in chronological order after your first run-through in Step 6. Set your timer for 15 minutes. **GO!**

Checklist
✓ _____
✓ _____
✓ _____
✓ _____
✓ _____

Each evening, prepare or preset the items on your list. Then check them off and add anything else that might help.

Gold Star!

Exercise 5b

Charting Your Progress: *Star Chart Tracking*

Seriously? Seriously! The Star Chart is your daily scorecard and reward tracker. While this ends up being most people's favorite part, for some it feels childish and unnecessary. I can't force you (darn), but after working with hundreds of clients, I strongly believe it is essential. It is also a *visual* tool and is simple and usually rewarding all on its own. You set it up at the beginning of the week, and then your primary job is to put stars in the boxes and make sure you give yourself the promised rewards.

At the end of each day, you get one shiny star in the Procrastination Doctor's Solution box for checking in, troubleshooting if necessary, immediately reinforcing your Time Block, and even shopping for future rewards AND partaking in your earned reward! In the Category box you get a star for completing your Time Block. When you have collected 6/7 stars in your first week, and 5/7 in weeks two through four in your Category box, you earn your chosen weekly reward.

Sample Star Chart for Fitness — Week One

The Procrastination Doctor's Solution	Check-in 6/7 days	Time Block about 8 minutes	Reward 24/28= Day at Spa	Day 1	Day 2	Day 3	Day 4	Day 5	Day 6	Day 7
Category: Fitness	6/7 blocks	5 minute blocks	Weekly Reward: 6/7 = Yearly Subscription to FitRadio							

Your Star Chart Template

The Procrastination Doctor's Solution	Check-in 6/7 days	Time Block about 8 minutes	Reward 24/28= Day at Spa	Day 1	Day 2	Day 3	Day 4	Day 5	Day 6	Day 7
Category:	6/7 blocks	_____ minute Time Blocks	Weekly Reward: 6/7 =							

After your four weeks, you may choose to do a Time Block only a few days a week, but while you form the habit in these first 28 days, aim for almost every day.

Just one more note on rewards: many of us feel guilty and conflicted when we spend money or time recreationally. By systematically giving yourself a predetermined (this is extremely important) reward if, and only if, you have done what you said (measured by input), you open yourself to an entirely new experience — the experience of earning and then enjoying a "guilty pleasure" guilt-free.

**Today I will pretend that I am famous and that everyone
I see is a shy, but adoring fan.
~ Ann Thornhill and Sarah Wells**

Step Six: It's Showtime!

Iron Out the Kinks
Technical Rehearsal
Dress Rehearsal
Curtain's Up!

THE FIRST WEEK OF your program will start gently—you get a tech rehearsal and a dress rehearsal to iron out any last-minute kinks before opening night.

Iron Out the Kinks

Day One: Technical Rehearsal

In the final week before a theatrical production opens, there is the technical rehearsal. It's a rehearsal for the lighting and sound technicians to make sure they know what needs to happen and when. It is also the time for the prop master to make sure all the props are in their right places. We never want to assume the stage manager can remember all our props, entrances, exits and costumes, so it's our responsibility to make sure she's got it all on the correct lists. Technical rehearsals are sort of boring for the actors because you don't do any action; you don't even get to say your lines—just the first word or two to make sure the lighting and sound technicians' notes line up just right with the script.

Day One of the Procrastination Doctor's Solution is a bit like a technical rehearsal. On this day, you will pretend you are actually going to do your bit, but you are really just making sure you have everything you need, in the right order, so you can act. Follow your checklist as closely as you can to determine if you've left anything out. Add any steps or supplies that would help it go well tomorrow. If you find that things are not in the most efficient and organic order, rearrange them during this Time Block or as soon as possible after you finish.

Checklist — Take Two

✓ _____

✓ _____

✓ _____

✓ _____

✓ _____

✓ _____

✓ _____

✓ _____

On Day One, aim for doing 1 minute of your Time Block in order to see if you have everything you will need. Stop. Use the rest of the time in your Time Block to revise your checklist and preset everything for tomorrow.

For Day One of your Procrastination Doctor's Solution check-in with your Star Chart, you get two stars: one for the minute you spent taking action and one for checking-in, putting a star on your chart, setting up the supplies and reinforcing for the next day.

Time Blocks

In your Time Block, you have the freedom to choose any action that matches your mood as long as it fits with your category and goals. This openness combats a great deal of resistance you might usually encounter. You probably have a fairly good idea what actions you should be taking. If not, use your time to research, brainstorm or reach out for suggestions. You can use the time to create a menu of options of things you could do, but think of them as a menu of options from which you can choose depending on your energy, mood, what you learned the previous day, etc.

Day Two: Final Dress Rehearsal

Often the final dress rehearsal is held for a small group of invited guests. This means that you are trying your darndest to do everything right, but in the event that something does go wrong, the consequences aren't dire. This is usually the last time the director will give notes, suggestions or changes. After these notes, you've got all the instruction you are going to get, and the rest you will learn and master as you go.

On Day Two, to the best of your ability, complete the full Time Block (whatever you calculated for week one). Make any tweaks to the checklist, POP reminder, trigger, or anchor based on today's experience. That's it! You have designed your own Procrastination Doctor's Solution routine!

Day Three: Curtain's Up!

You've rehearsed and made adjustments; now it's "Curtain's Up!" Do your thing. Take your bow. Give yourself a round of applause!

No, seriously, you get a standing ovation for getting this far. You have completed the entire set-up. There is nothing else for you to do except follow your personalized blueprint for creating the habit of consistently taking action toward an aspect of your life that really matters to you. By taking a little targeted action consistently over an extended length of time, you can accomplish great things.

**Do not be too timid and squeamish about your actions.
All life is an experiment.
— Ralph Waldo Emerson**

Step Seven: Make It Your Own

Take It Home
Days 1-3
Days 4-7

Take It Home: 28 Days

Week One

Days 1–3

In Part Two, The Procrastination Doctor's Solution, 95 percent of your attention and energy was on creating a plan that would free you from needing willpower and motivation to establish an automatic trigger to take consistent action aimed at improving one aspect of your life and the foundations of a routine that will support you over the long term. Only 5 percent was about getting short-term results.

In Part Three, Troubleshooting, 95 percent of your energy and attention will be focused on taking the actions that will get you immediate and enduring results. Each time you follow your habit sequence, you will be establishing new neural pathways to support you over time.

The first three days kicked off your Procrastination Doctor's Solution. In some ways, the rockier it was, the better, because your focus was on fine-tuning the specifics to make each day going forward easier.

Days 4–7: Keep It Going

In the remainder of your first week, your Time Block is likely to be too short for you to see visible results. However, it is important to keep your experience of taking action in your chosen category as palatable, easy and effortless as possible. You are probably disrupting an established routine and it might feel awkward and uncomfortable. You might also be going against a habit of avoidance, so each minute you go toward action instead of away, you are changing your neurochemistry. Your progress might be invisible to the naked eye, but it's real.

Week Two

In this second week, you will be doubling the amount of time you spend taking focused action. In week two, the routine should start to feel easier and you might already be tempted to drop the Star Chart. Don't! This simple little action can help you maintain great results.

A child originally learns to fasten a seatbelt with lots of praise. The habit is maintained and continually reinforced by the click it makes when fastened. It's a small action, but a mighty powerful one. And as the child grows, the click of the seatbelt maintains a habit that was established with praise. The visual record of your progress is also much more gratifying than you expect.

Week Three

Around week three, as your Time Block gets easier and the novelty wears off, boredom and overconfidence can kick in. Don't underestimate the challenge of continuing; keep up with your Star Chart! You might also hear that negative voice in your head saying, "This isn't doing enough, fast enough," and taunting you to quit. Hang in there, and consider making the reward a bit juicier this week!

Week Four

After 21 days of consistent practice, your routine should start to be established. A type of "muscle memory" is developing in the brain—this is when new neural pathways are built. As they get stronger, your path gets wider and smoother. Even if it grows over or develops potholes, it will always be there to be cleared and repaved.

Use your chart to check in daily, track your progress and earn your rewards! Fly, little bird, fly!

Here are four Star Chart templates that you can make your own!

Your Star Chart Template—Week One

The Procrastination Doctor's Solution	Check-in 6/7 days	Time Block about 8 minutes	Reward 24/28=	Day 1	Day 2	Day 3	Day 4	Day 5	Day 6	Day 7
Category:	6/7 blocks	_____ minute Time Blocks	Weekly Reward: 6/7 =							

My Weekly Prize

Week One Prize: _____

for completing six Time Blocks

Your Star Chart Template—Week Two

The Procrastination Doctor's Solution	Check-in 6/7 days	Time Block about 8 minutes	Reward 24/28=	Day 1	Day 2	Day 3	Day 4	Day 5	Day 6	Day 7
Category:	6/7 blocks	_____ minute Time Blocks	Weekly Reward: 6/7 =							

My Weekly Prize

Week Two Prize: _____

for completing five Time Blocks

Your Star Chart Template—Week Three

The Procrastination Doctor's Solution	Check-in 6/7 days	Time Block about 8 minutes	Reward 24/28=	Day 1	Day 2	Day 3	Day 4	Day 5	Day 6	Day 7
Category:	6/7 blocks	_____ minute Time Blocks	Weekly Reward: 6/7 =							
My Weekly Prize										

Week Three Prize: _____

for completing five Time Blocks

Your Star Chart Template—Week Four

The Procrastination Doctor's Solution	Check-in 6/7 days	Time Block about 8 minutes	Reward 24/28=	Day 1	Day 2	Day 3	Day 4	Day 5	Day 6	Day 7
Category:	6/7 blocks	_____ minute Time Blocks	Weekly Reward: 6/7 =							
My Weekly Prize										

Week Four Prize: _____

for completing five Time Blocks

I need a couch with a timer and an auto-eject feature.
Then spikes come out so I can't sit back down.

Troubleshooting

Getting to Your Time Block
Using Your Time Block
General Program

Part Three
Troubleshooting

Getting to Your Time Block

Obstacle

I feel physically paralyzed and unable to leave the couch/bed/chair.

Strategy

Inertia, I know it well. Remember Newton's law of motion?

- An object that is at rest will stay at rest unless an external force acts upon it.
- An object that is in motion will not change its velocity unless an external force acts upon it.

You'll need the help of an external force. If you are stuck, you need to move.

Try this:

Wiggle your fingers and toes. Touch your right hand to your left knee, then your left hand to your right knee.

Set a loud, annoying alarm on your phone to go off in 10 minutes and throw it across the room (onto a soft surface.) Once you are up to get it, keep moving!

The next time you go to the restroom or the kitchen, use the momentum to get to your starting position for your new habit. Grab your phone, place it face down where you need to be to start your new action. Allow the urge to check notifications to pull you to the right spot.

Place a reminder in these two places for next time, that is, "As long as you're up, go to your desk, not back to the couch."

Phone a friend and have him or her talk you through getting yourself to the right place.

You might need to "turn on" your brain (activate the frontal cortex) with peppy music, funny videos, a great visualization of how good you will feel when done, etc.

Obstacle

I keep getting to the end of my day realizing I forgot all about my plan to do my Time Block right before my anchor.

Strategy

Yep, that's common. After all, you are trying to remember to do something you don't do! Right now, get up and attach a reminder to your anchor that you will not be able to miss tomorrow. Make sure you remind yourself that you are only holding off participating in your usual activity for a few minutes.

Seriously, right now, go to your anchor and tie a ribbon to the coffeepot, tape your laptop shut, put a blanket over your TV or put your vitamins in a Ziploc in your coffee grounds. If you are struggling with major inertia, see above and ask Siri (or the Android equivalent) to remind you in an hour (or in 10 hours) to attach a reminder to your anchor. If you snooze the reminder, set another one. Ask your roommate to help, throw your dog's collar into the middle of the room—anything to remember to set yourself a reminder for tomorrow. The time involved in addressing this earns a program star for the day!

Obstacle

I'm getting to the Time Block and all ready to start, but the next thing I know I've done my anchor and have moved onto something else.

Strategy

Distraction is sneaky and happens fast! If you get thrown off track easily, you can get thrown back on just as easily! See the above answer for ideas. If you think it might be an unconscious avoidance technique, see the section in Part One on "Avoiding Avoidance" for more information. Gold star for setting up an anti-distraction strategy.

Obstacle

No, really, I don't have the time.

Strategy

This is a common obstacle to making progress on your most important goals. That's why this program is set up the way it is. Create the habit sequence now and add time when your schedule allows.

Start by cutting your Time Block in half. Halve it as many times as you need. Having a short block for a while is fine. You still earn stars toward your grand prize.

A 60-second Time Block will be enough to establish your trigger and reward. Keep decreasing your Time Block to the point that it's more trouble to rationalize it away than it is to do it.

There are plenty of stories of people who started their exercise program with a walk to the end of the block daily, or who started a committed meditation practice with just 1 minute every morning. Once you are in the habit of doing a little bit of something, you might be surprised how it just grows naturally. The most important part is finding the space in your day and introducing the habit into your life.

Obstacle
By the time I get to my anchor, I'm just too fried from the day and exhausted to do anything else.

Strategy
By the end of a day, we have often used up all our reserves to do the "right" (aka future-oriented) action. You might need a different anchor that comes earlier in your day.

Using Your Time Block

Obstacle

I'm getting to my anchor and really trying to do my action, but I just can't seem to start. My head feels foggy, and I get overwhelmed.

Strategy

First, I hope you have been giving yourself a star each time you tried to move the dial. It all counts! Just by facing this challenge and not running away from it, you are starting to generate a new neural path in your brain and starting to weaken the avoidance habit (for more information on this, check the section "Avoiding Avoidance" in Part One).

You might be unsure how to start or what to do first. Sometimes there is an invisible lurking decision to make. For example, you still haven't scheduled your annual check-up. As you get near the phone, you remember you don't really like that doctor and need to find a new one. That requires researching doctors and dealing with your insurance plan, so you get blocked, unsure if you should just schedule with this one for now and find a better doc next year.

Tomorrow, when you get to your Time Block, if you are still stuck, try this: Tell yourself, "I'm not going to do it today, period. But if I was going to do it today, (which I'm not!) or tomorrow, when I'm more in the mood, the first thing I need to do is _____." If it's something fairly simple, like locate the most recent version of your résumé, spend your allotted time doing a mini search.

Spare your "tomorrow self" that step. And if that's too much, leave yourself a note that points you in the right direction, that is, "begin looking for old résumé on backup drive from old computer." If you have a decision to make, write out your thoughts! Otherwise they can spin around in our minds, we decide, we forget we decided, or why we made that choice and start all over again.

Imagine you have a nine-year-old assistant. The next action step needs to be so well-defined, she will know exactly what to do without having to contact you for anything.

Obstacle
I feel willing but unable to start.

Strategy
If you find yourself in a horrible struggle to get yourself to get going, don't panic or give up. You can still earn your star by using the Time Block to plan for tomorrow, explore what is happening, and articulate your objections. Doing any of these counts toward your Time Block!

Use the following worksheet (or one of your own making) to suss out the obstacles that might be preventing you from starting. Then brainstorm possible strategies to try to offset the obstacle.

Example Obstacle: When I tried to go to the gym, I couldn't find a clean pair of socks. The thought of working out in dirty socks or sockless was disgusting, so I didn't go.

Example Strategy: Buy more socks (or do more laundry, but let's be real).

Once you have figured out a strategy to try, add the necessary items or steps to your Checklist.

Obstacles

Strategies

Obstacle

I feel able but unwilling. I get to my anchor and can identify the next step so a nine year old would know how to proceed, and still, nothing.

Strategy

Consider that your new habit might be more challenging than you initially thought, and you might want to adjust your Time Blocks accordingly. After a few days of 1 minute, you can test yourself with 2–3 minutes. But if that results in escape behavior again, back up to 1 minute.

Sometimes it can help to think about, metaphorically, just getting your hands in the mud. By this I mean, touch the objects involved even if you don't do anything useful with them yet. Stack the pile of unopened mail into a slightly neater pile, put the letter opener on top of the pile, move the weights from under the couch to the top of the chair or pop the workout DVD in and press play.

Obstacle

This is so weird—I won't even do a minute.

Strategy

If you have reduced the time to 1 minute and are still struggling, so how about a better reward, closer in time. Although it's easy to dismiss 1 minute as totally pointless, go ahead and try a really juicy reward.

Now is the time to practice extreme self-compassion. Imagine how you would teach a frightened puppy to come closer to you. The tiniest movement might have to be rewarded until the pup's brain has begun to associate safety and pleasure with moving in the desired direction and getting up close and personal to check out the new thing.

Also, engaging in the new behavior for any amount of time requires delaying gratification. With practice, it will get easier. Think of this practice like strength training for your brain.

Obstacle

I feel repelled — as though a force is stopping me from starting, as though two magnets are facing each other the wrong way.

Strategy

Good for you! You have made it to a place where you can directly address what might be stopping you (in a gentle, nonthreatening way). Set a notebook and pen down near the place you are supposed to get down to business. Tomorrow, when you get there, use the allotted time for some detective work. Start an Objections Page. The time you spend doing this earns you a program star. You might need to voice your objections for a few days before you can respond to them. Often the mere identification of the block is enough. If not, treat yourself gently and see if you can talk yourself through, in writing, the way you might talk to a young child dealing with the same feelings.

Examples of Common Objections

Push back: I don't want to, I don't have to, you can't make me!

Fear: What if I actually do this? If I finish, I might have to . . .

Efficiency concerns: I don't think this is the best use of my time. It doesn't make sense to do it now; I'll do it later. Right now, I need to . . .

Existential crisis: Life is too short to spend it doing this. I'd rather be doing . . .

Obstacles: I can't because . . .

Write your own objections.

_____

_____

_____

_____

_____

_____

Obstacle
I feel anxious.

Strategy

Decrease the number of minutes of your new behavior to as few as necessary to get over the hurdle. Exposure in small doses helps you can get used to facing the dragon (see "Avoiding Avoidance" in Part One). Also, with small units of time, any results you achieve are less likely to trigger any possible fears, giving you less reason to feel anxious about starting. Even 1 minute helps you break the pattern and establishes a placeholder that you can widen with time. Just 1 minute earns your program and your action stars.

Obstacle

I give up. Absolutely nothing seems to be working, and I don't feel it's worth trying anymore, because nothing ever works for me.

Strategy

That's a hard place to be and kudos to you for even trying this program. Take a look at the early section on "Learned Helplessness" in Part One.

If doing 1 minute of your new action followed by a juicy reward still feels like it's beyond your resources at the moment, you might consider the help of therapist. It is possible more contributing to your stuck-ness than you can unravel alone.

But don't give up.

I've worked with many, many clients who started at this same place and went on to have happy productive lives. In fact, I worked with one client recently, who spent day after day smoking marijuana, watching television and surfing the Web. When we started our work together, he felt unable/unwilling to do anything differently. Eventually, he was able to play drums, his passion, for 60 seconds a day before turning on the television. The rest, as they say, was history. Last I heard, he had a fulltime job, a girlfriend and his apartment was clean.

GENERAL PROGRAM

Obstacle
I'm having an existential crisis about whether this is worth it.

Strategy
The exercises break things way down and you might not need to do them. If the program, and the exercises look complicated or unwieldy, consider skipping the exercises and doing your best to fill out the Big Payoff boxes—I have designed it just for this.

Also, doubt is to be expected when that initial spark of motivation and determination (and misery) subsides. In Appendix One are exercises that you can do within your Time Block. These can be especially useful to explore if doing this is worth your time, energy and money. If you decide it is, consider offering yourself a much grander Grand Prize—pronto—before this crops up again.

Obstacle
I got partway through and now something urgent and important has come up. I just don't have time to keep doing this, let alone to add time.

Strategy
If you run out of time for the full Time Block, always, always, always do at least 3 minutes of it to keep it locked in! Let go of all the other habits if something disruptive happens in your life, and keep 3–5 minutes of your new behavior until things calm down again. If you successfully complete all the actions in your routine, give yourself a prize.

Obstacle

I shouldn't need a reward. Just doing my Time Block makes me feel good and should be rewarding enough.

Strategy

We procrastinate more on tasks without immediate rewards. If we did sit-ups and saw the results, it would be easier. After a while, the action might feel rewarding in and of itself. Until then, you might need a much juicier treat, now.

Knowing how good or bad we will feel for doing or not doing something doesn't get us to start. The internal motivation mechanism feels as though it's broken. This is why there is such a huge emphasis in this program on external rewards to motivate you to do something long enough that motivation is no longer required.

And give yourself the promised daily reinforcers! Your stars and this strategic ordering of activities might be all you need to keep yourself going. But if you slip for three days in a row, it's clear that you need a better incentive. Go back to your rewards list or Dear Santa letter and identify rewards that work for you.

Give yourself an immediate reward each time. It can be a symbolic, inexpensive treat such as lighting a fragrant candle, using the good body wash instead of the Ivory soap, upgrading to organic milk, etc. The important thing is to stay motivated, whatever it takes!

Obstacle

Routine makes me feel too robotic, and I get bored.

Strategy

That's a common thought—before people do it. The surprise is how really wonderful the program starts to feel, especially when you are calling all the shots and choosing what to do with your life. Structure in a small part of your day liberates huge blocks of guilt-free unstructured time. You actually will probably get more of what you want.

Obstacle

I'm not sure I'm doing everything right. It almost seems too easy.

Strategy

Perfectionism might be creeping in. Experiment with not doing things the right way or the best way or even a good way. Just do them in some way.

Obstacle

My anchor keeps moving.

Strategy

That's fine, your sequence isn't tied to a time of day. Your Time Block can just move with it.

Obstacle

I can't postpone my anchor long enough to do something before it.

Strategy

Strengthen your brain, the same way you would strengthen a bicep. The ability to delay gratification can be developed.

The most successful anchors come after the new action. You might need to do a little rearranging. If you tried "coming in the front door after work" as your anchor, and you can't put your action before that, then find something that usually happens right after that. Go to the fridge. Pet the dog. Change clothes. Turn on the TV. Put dishes away (hey, it could happen for some people)!

Obstacle

My goal is not measurable by time—but by accomplishing something in particular.

Strategy

This is how we have been conditioned to think about tasks—by accomplishment and completion. If it is actually impossible to set a Time Block for this habit, you might want to choose a different new behavior for your first goal to get familiar with this method.

Obstacle

I'm not really suffering anymore with the issue I started with.

Strategy

Feel free to take on a different challenge. Or, take a look at the motivational exercises at the top of this section. Remind yourself of why you originally wanted to form this new habit.

Obstacle

I'm never going to get anywhere at this rate! Do I really have to stop?

Strategy

You might be starting with 5 minutes a day. And yes, you need to stop (see "Bottling the Magic of Deadlines" in Part Two). But this program might only be taking 10 minutes of your day, max, in the beginning. You still have the whole rest of your day to do things your normal way. If you want to go on a cleaning binge or spend a weekend on your screenplay, go right ahead!

Obstacle

I missed a day! I've ruined my 21-day streak and have to start again.

Strategy

You don't have to do 21 days in a row. There is no magic number—that's just a guideline. Every time you do it, you are making it easier for the next time. Even if that next time is next year.

Obstacle

I set up the program, then got distracted.

Strategy

Don't panic and don't beat yourself up! You are in this for the long run. If you spent five days trying to get yourself to walk around the block, but haven't, you haven't earned the stars for your action. However, if you have spent a teeny bit of time trying, you HAVE earned your program stars. This is building a habit.

If you haven't done anything, or even tried, this might not be the right time. Save all your hard work setting up and come back to it when the time is right. You can jump right in next time.

The goal is 24 repetitions of your new habit in a 28 day period or until it starts feeling automatic. They don't have to be consecutive days, and 24 out of 28 is an arbitrary guideline. The more often you practice your action sequence, the easier it gets.

When you realize that you have missed a day, take a breath, thank yourself for checking in and recommit to your next Time Block. Remember, you are doing this to make your life better. Being hard on yourself doesn't work nearly as well as being kind (and strategic).

Obstacle
I'm feeling sabotaged by people close to me.

Strategy
When you make a change, the people in your life might need some time to adapt. They might have some fears of their own. There is often a fear of abandonment underneath sabotage so reassuring them that they matter to you, and will continue to matter, might help.

Try to give them a specific and fairly easy task to support you. This can help them feel connected to you.

Obstacle
My husband/wife/partner/sister/parent thinks this is ridiculous and/or believes I will fail.

Strategy
Go ahead and be successful anyway. You deserve it.
One of my favorite Chinese proverbs is:
   "Those who say it cannot be done should not interrupt the person doing it."

We are what we repeatedly do.
Excellence, then, is not an act, but a habit.

~Aristotle

Beyond 28 Days

Gamble on Your Future
Habitus Interruptus
Add Another Habit
Final Thoughts

Part Four
Maintenance and Beyond Your 28 Days

Gamble on Your Future

To learn a new behavior, you need to reward it immediately every single time it happens. But to maintain a behavior after it has been established, take a cue from the casinos.

Something becomes addictive when the payoff comes at completely random intervals. In the lab you will see rats repeatedly pressing a lever in hopes of getting a pellet. At the slot machines, you will see people repeatedly pulling the lever in hopes of getting, well, basically a pellet.

Look back at your list of rewards from Step Four. Cut out 28 slips of paper. Put rewards (by name) on 10 of the slips. Put all the slips in a bag. Each time over the next four weeks that you complete your Time Block, choose a slip. Make sure the rewards are worth it. And make sure you give yourself the reward! I recommend having a supply of unopened goodies on hand; you still want the reward to be as immediate as possible.

Habitus Interruptus

Life happens and your carefully cultivated habits are likely to get disrupted at some point. It goes without saying that you want to haul yourself back onto the wagon as soon as you can. Hang onto all the work you have done here. You now have a blueprint for reinstating that habit from scratch. You'll never again have to figure out the process and the little details that made it easier. Follow your blueprint exactly with new enticing rewards. If you've been off the wagon for a while, start with small Time Blocks! If you were running 10 miles a day and then sprained your ankle, your doctor would probably recommend starting with short stints and building back up. And your procrastination doctor is recommending, strongly, the same thing.

Add Another Habit

My ultimate goal with the Procrastination Doctor's Solution is to show you a technique to create the life you have always known is possible. If you have been consistently taking action in one area of your life, you might already be noticing a positive snowball effect in other areas. For example, if you chose to focus on increasing your level of fitness, you might have found that you are eating better or that you have more energy at the end of the day to play with your kids.

If you are ready to add another new habit, you can go back to "Exercise 1c: Finalists" from Step One for some ideas. Don't feel you need to tackle a category that is emotionally loaded, super tedious or complex, and/or overwhelming, if your life still feels more chaotic than managed. Usually after habit number two is established and has been practiced for 21 days, this balance shifts, and, almost magically, it will feel possible to tackle the tougher aspects of your life. Hang in there!

Use the exercises in Part Two to add new habits, building separate Time Blocks for each habit or linking them together to create a chain.

In either case, your next habit must start small — probably no more than 5 minutes to start. Starting small is humbling and slows progress in the beginning, I know. I will save you a LOT of time and frustration if you will just trust me on this, put your pride aside, and do only 1 minute if you have to!

If you feel really crunched for time, you might choose to borrow 10 minutes from the habit you just developed and donate half to the new habit and the other half toward learning to balance multiple priorities by attending to the program and your Star Chart.

Keeping the Two Habits Separate

To create a separate Time Block, repeat the process that you just completed: find a new anchor at a time that makes sense for this new action, locate the trigger, and develop a stand-alone formula for the new habit.

Habit #1: **Trigger** ☐ First Behavior Time Block ☐ Reward ☐**Anchor**
Habit #2: **Trigger** ☐ Second Behavior Time Block ☐ Reward ☐ **Anchor**

Connecting Two Habits

You can link Habit Two to Habit One and begin creating a chain or a routine.

Trigger ☐ First Time Block ☐ Reward
Second Time Block ☐ Reward ☐ **Anchor**

If you decide to link Habits One and Two together, insert the new habit into the sequence using the same trigger and anchor from your first Time Block. Put the new, fledgling, habit after your more established Time Block. For example, if you set up "play drums" before checking Facebook and after your morning coffee, put "job search" after "play drums" unless drum playing has become solid enough to serve as an anchor. Putting the new one first sets up too much potential for abandoning the whole string if job hunting turns out to be problematic and playing drums is contingent on it.

When you have successfully completed 5 minutes of each category for at least six days, add 5 more minutes to your goal for each category. If you want or need to wait longer before adding more time, take longer! It's better to go too slow than too fast.

There is nothing new to learn here—you have all the tools. Your Star Chart will now go from two rows to three or more, depending on how many habits you are adding.

If You Have an Unstructured Life

This program was originally designed for just this situation. If you have large or infinite blocks of time with no one watching and virtually no immediate consequences for not completing things, you might need more structure and now might want to develop more than one new Time Block. Choose no more than three areas to address. The Time Blocks can be free-floating and done in any order.

The fun (okay, I'm a little geeky about this stuff) is when you can turn an anchor for one action into a trigger for another. If you used "finishing breakfast" to trigger "daily planning," which is anchored with your second cup of coffee, then getting the second cup of coffee can be used to trigger "working on your novel" which is then anchored by "checking Twitter."

If you don't make it for a day, that's fine. You should have at least one day off per week. You might need to change the order or find another anchor and create a separate Time Block sequence for your second habit.

If you put Habit Two after Habit One and you never got to it because you couldn't focus that long or the anchor really belonged after Habit One, try putting Habit Two first but only for a brief Time Block. If you don't get to Habit One twice, abandon ship and find a new anchor and trigger for the new habit. I recommend first trying the new sequence after the one you have just carefully cultivated in case you run out of time or energy. You made it Priority #1 for a reason. But this stuff isn't in stone. Experiment with what works for you.

After two unsuccessful attempts to add another habit, refer to the troubleshooting section of this book for more solutions that might apply.

POP Reminder and Checklist

As you add new habits to your daily routine, you are going to expand your Checklist and set up POP reminders as necessary. Give your brain a break and prepare for each new habit as thoroughly as you did for the first habit.

Juggling

One of the struggles I hear from clients is the challenge of maintaining balance. While giving one thing a lot of our attention and time, other important things seem to get neglected until they reach a crisis level and then our focus shifts and the trouble repeats.

I know this pattern well, and it is letting everything else slide during times of singular focus that causes much of the chaos in our lives.

If this applies to you, but you need to develop multiple habits simultaneously, your top priority, your new behavior, the one thing that you don't let slide, is this program.

You are already accustomed to checking in with your chart daily — that is a habit you have already formed. Now you will still be checking in daily but managing multiple areas. If you can only really focus on one thing, focus on earning a star in the Procrastination Doctor's Solution box by using the program management tools: checklist, Star Chart, and rewards. Learn to juggle this way and you can build balance into your life.

Final Thoughts

If you have gotten here, you have set up your own behavior modification program! It took some work, but you should be close to automatically and consistently making progress on your goals. The real point of all this, though, is to eliminate as much of the time that you spend not doing what you intended to do and to stop feeling guilty for most of that time. Now you can do those activities and enjoy them. Paradoxically, most people find that without the to-do list looming over their day, they choose different activities in their down time.

Leisure time ideally is guilt-free! Most of my clients cannot fathom that idea. When you complete your target Time Blocks, *consider* that you have done enough for one day. Usually we can only be focused and productive for a part of the day, and the idea of the Time Blocks is to become as efficient as possible in a limited amount of time. And once you have reached that limit, that's good enough for now.

There is always tomorrow and you can trust that tomorrow you will also get things done. So go to the beach, curl up with your Kindle (that just sounds wrong), stare off into space (if that's as fun for you as it is for me) and relax. Give yourself a break from the constant internal battle to be productive. A first step is to practice deliberately not being productive for at least 30 minutes. It might just be way more challenging than you think.

A client once told me that she was terrible at taking breaks that actually refreshed her. She said it was as though she spent her days paddling a canoe, and when she got too tired to continue, she would pull the canoe onto the shore. However, instead of getting out and lying in the sun, she would sit in the dry-docked canoe and keep paddling at the air. That didn't do much to rejuvenate her.

When you rest, get out of your canoe and leave the paddle behind. It's not going anywhere. And you will row farther and faster and onto greater discoveries after you have rested.

Well, dear reader, I've done it! It took many years, but these ideas are finally out of my head (and off a trillion disorganized pieces of paper and computer files) and available to you! It's not perfect, but if I had waited for that, well, you wouldn't be reading this.

Brilliant, funny, summarizing and inspiring concluding paragraph coming soon—

Appendices

Appendix One
Supplies and Supplemental Exercises

Timer: You'll need a timer that counts down and ideally gives warning alerts at 5 and 10 minutes. Those mentioned below are about $10 and gives warnings 5 and 10 minutes before the end.

http://www.wayfair.com/EKCO-5.5-Digital-Timer-1094966-EKC1234.html

http://www.walmart.com/ip/Classic-Digital-Timer/38241735

Supplemental Exercises

Motivation Insurance: Slip, Sliding, Away

In the beginning I discussed how our energy and enthusiasm to change are finite and therefore we want to use them well. In addition to setting up a system that rewards your ongoing efforts, here are some exercises you can do to capture your determination so that you can access it later.

Use these exercises to document your commitment and have them available to remotivate you and get you back on track with your Procrastination Doctor's Solution. Do any of them that interest you or create your own exercises. You can do them during your Time Block or at other times. Refer back to them as time passes and your initial enthusiasm wanes.

Exercise 1: Motivation Exploration

Time limit: 5 minutes

Spend 5 minutes writing out thoughts in response to these questions:

- Why do you want to make positive, lasting changes?
- What will make this time different from the past?
- What will be the benefits of making these changes and sticking to them?

Exercise 2: What Is It Costing You Not to Change?

Time limit: 15 minutes

In this exercise, you are going to guesstimate how much neglecting this area of your life is currently costing you in time, money and psychic units of energy.

Think about each of the following and write down, for each category, at least three ways that not changing is costing you. Set your timer for 15 minutes. **GO!**

1. Time

Examples

20 minutes/week looking for keys.

70 minutes/week returning home for something I forgot.

60 minutes/week trying to exercise off calories from emotional eating.

2. Money

Examples

$10/month in expired grocery coupons.

$40/month for not paying credit card bill on time.

$40/week eating out instead of taking lunch to work.

$300/month for clients/accounts I might have if I had been more organized.

$680/year for cavities I could have avoided by flossing regularly.

3. Psychic Units of Energy

Examples

1 unit/day worrying about the dying plants I never get around to watering.

4 units/day worrying about not having Cloud storage for my data.

15 units/day brainstorming excuses for not returning calls and emails.

25 units/day worrying about how my bad habits will leave me penniless.

30 units/day feeling shame about what's not getting done.

At the end of the 15 minutes, add up the time per day, week and year that you are spending by not committing to your new habit. Weigh that number against your Time Block commitment to truly evaluate whether you don't have enough time to make a change.

Exercise 3: Visions of Success

Time limit: 10 minutes

Set your timer for 10 minutes.

In this exercise, you are going to think about someone you really admire, someone who already practices the habits you want. It could be a lean, fit friend; a movie star you love; or perhaps Martha Stewart, the emblem of efficiency. It could even be someone you resent—whatever works for you.

I imagine my friend, Mary. She must have been born with the habits of picking up after herself, being neat, organized and on time. I admire and respect Mary, so when I really want to go to bed with my clothes on the floor and my teeth unbrushed, I think, "What would Mary do?" With her as my guide, the answer is always clear. Throughout the day, I imagine what she would do with a sink full of dishes and her favorite show about to start.

Post a reminder of this person in a spot you're likely to come across every day.

It could be a photograph, a quotation or just a name written on a slip of paper. You could post it on your mirror, by your kitchen sink, by the front door or even make it your computer's wallpaper—as long as you'll be reminded of your role model on a daily basis.

Exercise: "Creative-ational" Writing

Time limit: 5 minutes

Choose any of these quick writing exercises to pep yourself up. They are great to look at later for a quick reminder.

- Write yourself a pep talk for later, when your heart just isn't in it. Imagine yourself coaching a good friend as you do this.
- Eat your heart out! A brief note announcing your success to your competitor.
- "Dear Naysayer" letter: a brief note announcing your success to someone who said you'd never make it.
- Visualize your ideal space and self and write the profile you would like to read about it/you.
- Write the school bulletin announcement you'd love to send to the alumni association.
- "When I get there, I will . . . buy _____ / tell _____ / read about myself in _____."
- "When I was there before, I felt . . . _____."

If writing doesn't work for you because you are a more visual or auditory person, try these variations of the above writing exercises.

- Make a vision board with pictures and drawings: How do you want to look and feel? What will your life look like?
- Record yourself talking about how great you feel when you're on track and maybe how awful you feel when you're not.
- Find a song that reminds you of how you will feel when you are on track.

Appendix Two: Worksheets

Ready, Set, Go!

Sign this contract with yourself or, if you can't reach a pen, text yourself. If you are feeling particularly brave, tell someone else.

I, _____, *will give myself* _____

for setting up my program and then checking in 24 out of 28 days.

I, _____, will give myself

_____

when I complete this 28 day program.

Date: _____

Time: _____

Signature: _____

Exercise 1b: Piling System

Job and Career	Finances	Health and Fitness	Diet and Nutrition
Creativity	Spiritual	Family and Friends	Intimate Relationships
Personal Growth	Home Environment	Office Environment	Miscellaneous

Exercise 1c: Finalists

Set your timer for 1 minute. **GO!**

1. _____

2. _____

3. _____

4. _____

Exercise 1d: The Big Kahuna

The Big Payoff
The category in which I most want to make change right now is:
Give it a fun, playful, appealing name if you want.

Exercise 2a: Success Time

My Category is: _____

My TARGET goal is to work on my category for

_____**minutes/hours/day**

Exercise 2b: Training Schedule

The Big Payoff

End Goal: _____ min/day

Week 1: minutes = 25% of your target = _____min

Week 2: minutes = 50% of your target = _____min

Week 3: minutes = 75% of your target = _____min

Week 4: minutes = 100% of your target = _____min

In week one, my goal is to focus on _____ **for** _____ **minutes a day.**

Exercise 3a: Anchor List

Think through your typical day or week and write down activities you do consistently, however small, that could possibly be used as an anchor. Don't edit yourself at this point—just write down everything that comes to mind. Set your timer for 6 minutes. **GO!**

_____

_____

_____

_____

_____

Exercise 3d: Find Your Trigger and Make a Sandwich

Time limit: 3 minutes

Think about your anchor and what you do immediately before starting it.

Before I _____ (write in anchor),

I _____ (trigger).

Your Time Block goes between these two events.

Exercise 3e: POP Reminder

Think about a POP reminder that will remind you to do your Time Block. Where does the reminder have to be located so that you do not overlook or ignore it?

My POP reminder is _____.

The Big Payoff: Action Sequence and Reminders	
My Time Block is:	_____ minutes a day
Focusing on:	
My anchor is:	
My trigger is:	
My POP reminder will be:	
My reminder to set my POP is:	

~133~

Exercise 4b: The Chosen Few

My Four Weekly Prizes

Week One Prize: _____

for completing six Time Blocks

Week Two Prize: _____

for completing five Time Blocks

Week Three Prize: _____

for completing five Time Blocks

Week Four Prize: _____

for completing five Time Blocks

Exercise 4d: Promises, Promises

Grand Prize

The Grand Prize I promise to give myself for tracking my progress for 24 out of 28 days is:

_____

Exercise 4e: The Whole Shebang

I am creating change in this area of my life:

_____

****

I aim to take action on it for _____ minutes on most days.

****

I will start automatically after this trigger: _____. My reminder will

be _____, and I will put it/create it

by_____.

****

My anchor is: _____.

Each time I complete my Time Block, I will reinforce my action by getting

_____ or doing _____.

****

When I finish one week, I will reward myself with:

_____.

****

For successfully completing 24 out of 28 days, I earn this Grand Prize

_____.

Exercise 5a: Checklist, Take One

Checklist
✓ _____
✓ _____
✓ _____
✓ _____
✓ _____

Exercise 5b: A Star Is Born

Your Star Chart Template

The Procrastination Doctor's Solution	Check-in 6/7 days	Time Block about 8 minutes	Reward 24/28= Day at Spa	Day 1	Day 2	Day 3	Day 4	Day 5	Day 6	Day 7
Category:	6/7 blocks	_____ minute Time Blocks	Weekly Reward: 6/7 =							

Step 6: Iron Out the Kinks

Checklist — Take Two

✓ _____

✓ _____

✓ _____

✓ _____

✓ _____

✓ _____

✓ _____

✓ _____

Step 7: Make It Your Own

Your Star Chart Template — Week One

The Procrastination Doctor's Solution	Check-in 6/7 days	Time Block about 8 minutes	Reward 24/28=	Day 1	Day 2	Day 3	Day 4	Day 5	Day 6	Day 7
Category:	6/7 blocks	_____ minute Time Blocks	Weekly Reward: 6/7 =							
My Weekly Prize										

Week One Prize: _____

for completing six Time Blocks

Your Star Chart Template — Week Two

The Procrastination Doctor's Solution	Check-in 6/7 days	Time Block about 8 minutes	Reward 24/28=	Day 1	Day 2	Day 3	Day 4	Day 5	Day 6	Day 7
Category:	6/7 blocks	_____ minute Time Blocks	Weekly Reward: 6/7 =							
My Weekly Prize										

Week Two Prize: _____

for completing five Time Blocks

Your Star Chart Template — Week Three

The Procrastination Doctor's Solution	Check-in 6/7 days	Time Block about 8 minutes	Reward 24/28=	Day 1	Day 2	Day 3	Day 4	Day 5	Day 6	Day 7
Category:	6/7 blocks	_____ minute Time Blocks	Weekly Reward: 6/7 =							
My Weekly Prize										
Week Three Prize: _____ for completing five Time Blocks										

Your Star Chart Template — Week Four

The Procrastination Doctor's Solution	Check-in 6/7 days	Time Block about 8 minutes	Reward 24/28=	Day 1	Day 2	Day 3	Day 4	Day 5	Day 6	Day 7
Category:	6/7 blocks	_____ minute Time Blocks	Weekly Reward: 6/7 =							
My Weekly Prize										
Week Four Prize: _____ for completing five Time Blocks										

Part Three: Troubleshooting

Obstacles

Solutions

Appendix Three: Changes and Categories

Examples

Changes

- Get in shape.
- Make more money.
- Get organized.
- Run a 5K.
- Write a novel.
- Become famous.
- Meet my true love.
- Get out of debt.
- Lose 10 pounds.
- Be nicer to my sister.
- Make some new friends.
- Stop being so messy.
- Get out of bed earlier.
- Make the bed.
- Floss daily.
- Stop losing my keys.
- Clean up my office.
- Shred the boxes of paper.
- Remember Grandma's birthday.
- Eat healthier food.
- Drink more water.
- Pay bills on time.
- Write every day.

Categories

Here are several **categories** that might inspire some ideas:

- Job and career
- Finances
- Health and fitness
- Diet and nutrition
- Creativity
- Spirituality
- Family and friends
- Intimate relationships
- Personal growth
- Home environment
- Office environment
- Miscellaneous

Appendix Four: Incentives by Category

Office Organization

- a professional organizer
- an app that scans receipts
- new file folders
- pens
- three-hole punch
- index cards
- notebooks
- good printer paper
- printer/scanner combo
- planner
- desk accessories
- comfortable desk chair
- handsome file cabinet
- a nice lamp
- permission to not check email for a specified period of time

Mental Health

- call a friend
- snuggle with your pet turtle
- session with a hypnotherapist
- guided imagery recording
- meditation class, app

Home

- fragrant candle
- glowers
- a fresh sponge
- new rubber gloves
- better cleaning products
- good scrub brush
- new shower curtain
- dimmer switch for lights
- new lamp
- new pillows
- new mattress
- matching accessories
- subscription to home magazine or a flower service
- new cabinets
- closet sorters
- wooden hanger
- professional closet overhaul
- cleaning service
- window washer
- dinner party at your place
- new dishes/plates/glassware

Health

- special tea
- water filter
- organic foods
- exotic fruit
- healthy smoothie
- department store facial

- new grooming products
- body scrub
- self-tanning cream
- nutritionist

Fitness

- Fitbit or other fitness device
- premium subscription to fitness app
- new athletic socks, shoes
- workout clothes
- fitness video
- subscription to fitness magazine
- spinning/yoga/martial arts/dance class
- new workout music
- personal trainer
- fat testing
- new scale

Career

- smartphone
- computer
- software
- iPad
- trip to office supply store
- writing coach
- new business cards
- assistant
- standing desk

Pamper

- massage
- wearing the good cologne
- nice lotion
- special jewelry even though it's not a special occasion
- watching TV
- reading a good book or the sports pages
- sleeping in, sitting in the sun
- manicure/pedicure
- trip to the spa
- shopping
- MP3 player, new car stereo
- car accessories
- professional carwash
- personal shopper

Play

- a day at a local sports bar/restaurant watching a game
- sailing lessons
- hanging out with a friend
- playing a video game
- surfing the Web
- movie or theater tickets
- a trip to the park/lake/museum/beach/mountains
- a weekend away
- a trip overseas with a friend or lover
- downloading new music
- lunch with friends
- test drive a sports car

Acknowledgments

I have been working on this over such an extended period of years, that I am certainly forgetting extremely important people, but here goes, in alphabetical order (because anything else could take another week!) Maurissa Afanador, Jill Badonsky, Mary Burch, Vera Eck, Willow Evans, Jill Hangen, Elaine Hatfield, Robin Lewis, Mindy Katz, Kim Murphy, Kristine Oller, my parents — Carin Rapson and Richard Rapson, Mary Samson, Linda Roggli, Ari Tuckman, Joni Wilson, Barbara Winstead, all the program participants over the years, all the clients who shared their struggles and solutions with me, all the participants of my presentations who said — "Finish the book, we want it!" and, of course, out of alphabetical order, Pita, Piper and now, Tazzy.

Thank You

Thank you for reading my book.

If you enjoyed it, please take a moment to leave me a review.

About the Author

Kim Kensington grew up in Hawaii and went to high school with US President Barack Obama. After receiving her bachelor of arts degree in psychology at Amherst College in Massachusetts, she earned her doctorate in clinical psychology from the Virginia Consortium Program in Psychology. An actor and psychologist in private practice in Los Angeles, California, Kim is known as The Procrastination Doctor. She has spent more than 20 years researching, testing, and creating solutions to overcome procrastination for her patients. Recognizing the need for an "out of the box" process, she developed this program. Kim, a member of CHADD and ADDA, regularly lectures and performs stand-up comedy about procrastination and adult ADHD for international audiences. She lives in Santa Monica, California, with her dog, Tazzy, who keeps her on a very tight schedule.

Connect with Me

Facebook

The Procrastination Doctor

Website

http://www.procrastinationdoctor.com/

Email

kim@procrastinationdoctor.com

LinkedIn

https://www.linkedin.com/in/kimkensington